Dear PaPa,

Merry Christmas.

When I saw this book I thought of you!

Love,
Eve

1985 x-mas

Illustrated
History of
Aircraft

Illustrated History of Aircraft

Edited by Brendan Gallagher

GALLERY BOOKS
An Imprint of W. H. Smith Publishers Inc.
112 Madison Avenue
New York City 10016

CONTENTS

First published in Great Britain by Octopus Books Limited
59 Grosvenor Street, London W1

This edition published in 1984 by Gallery Books
An imprint of W.H. Smith Publishers Inc.
112 Madison Avenue, New York, New York 10016

ISBN 0 8317 4867 2

Printed in Hong Kong

Chapter 1
BEGINNINGS

NO single invention has changed the world and the lives of men as much as the aeroplane. Yet the realization of man's age-old yearning to share the lofty domain of the birds came only at the turn of our own century. Through countless ages before this, great men and eccentrics had speculated, prophesied and experimented with all manner of devices. Leonardo da Vinci made numerous sketches for man-powered ornithopters in the 15th century, and also proposed the helicopter and parachute. None were built, however, and his belief that man could fly by his own muscle-power was ill-founded, as was to be proved by Giovanni Alphonso Borelli, a professor of mathematics at Messina and Pisa, in *De Motu Animalium*, published in 1680 after his death.

Man's first essays into the atmosphere were made by hot-air balloon. The first person to conceive of this means of ascension was a Brazilian

Jesuit priest, Father Bartolomeu de Gusmao. On August 8, 1709, he demonstrated a model hot-air balloon before King John V and Queen Maria Anna of Portugal, papal nuncio Cardinal Conti and a host of dignitaries.

Reports of Gusmao's attempt to fly are vague and, although he foresaw its military potential, his discovery was forgotten. The world had to wait another 74 years for the Montgolfier brothers, Etienne and Joseph, to restate the principle all over again. Their first public demonstration took place at Annonay, near Lyons, France, on June 4, 1783. By the time a full-size 'Montgolfière' had taken the first man aloft in Paris on November 21, 1783, Professor J. A. C. Charles, another Frenchman, had already begun work on the first hydrogen-filled balloon. This ascended from Paris on 1 December the same year, carrying its designer and a Mr Robert. Ballooning caught on rapidly, the first flight in Britain following on September 15, 1784,

and meetings and exhibitions became popular social events.

The initial outburst of enthusiasm was quickly followed by the realization that the aeronaut had no control over his aerial peregrinations. Consequently a lot of effort, both mental and physical, was expended in vain attempts to direct these passive spheres with oars, sails and hand-driven propellers. The answer, of course, lay in the steerable airship. But although the French officer General Meusnier designed a craft of this type in 1784, it was not until 1852 that French engineer Henri Giffard flew the first practical airship.

The shortcomings of the balloon as a means of aerial navigation were very obvious. But before a practical heavier-than-air aircraft could be produced, belief in flapping-wing flight had to be

abandoned. The key lay in divorcing the thrust mechanism from the lift-producing system, in envisaging a bird in gliding flight with its wings stationary, and then adding an independent means of propulsion.

The man who finally hit upon this was the Englishman Sir George Cayley, who in a long and intensely active life (1773–1857) was to provide the foundations of modern aeronautics. As Cayley saw it, the problem was 'to make a surface support a given weight by the application of power to the resistance of air'. By 1799 he had understood the need to balance the forces of lift, drag and thrust, and in 1804 he turned a simple kite into a successful model glider 1.5 m (5 ft) long and equipped with an adjustable cruciform tail surface. Five years later a full-sized glider with a wing area of 18.58 m² (200 sq ft) was flown successfully, and the same year *Nicholson's Journal* published his triple paper 'On Aerial Navigation', in which were laid out the basic principles of flight control and aerodynamics.

Later in life Cayley built full-sized triplane gliders, the first making brief hops in 1849 with ballast and a small-boy passenger aboard. The second carried his unwilling coachman aloft on the first genuine manned gliding flight in history in 1853.

Cayley's list of achievements is too great to present here, but his one failing was a preference for propulsive flappers rather than propellers, even

Above Tested twice in 1897, the Frenchman Clement Ader's third full-size aircraft, *Avion III,* powered by two steam engines, failed to fly.

Right One of the dozen non-rigid airships built in France by the French-domiciled Brazilian pioneer, Alberto Santos-Dumont, between 1898 and 1907.

though he was completely familiar with the latter and proposed their use in dirigible airships. He understood streamlining, the technique of bird flight, the lifting effect of a cambered aerofoil, and was the first man to suggest the use of an internal-combustion engine (using gunpowder) to propel an aeroplane.

In 1843 the imagination of the people was captured by a prophetic design for an 'Aerial Steam Carriage', born in the fertile mind of William Samuel Henson of Chard, Somerset. The ambitious Henson proposed a wire-braced monoplane spanning 45.72 m (150 ft) and propelled by two pusher propellers driven by a 25–30 hp steam engine in the fuselage. Featuring a tricycle undercarriage and double-surfaced wings, it was never built, but exciting engravings of the machine flying over exotic countries continued to appear in print well into the next century.

Helped by his friend John Stringfellow, Henson built a model spanning 6.09 m (20 ft) and tested it at Bala Down, near Chard, during 1845 to 1847. The model proved incapable of sustained flight after launch down a ramp, and Henson abandoned the

idea. Undismayed, Stringfellow went on to produce another monoplane powered by an improved steam engine. This was launched from an overhead wire in a shed in Chard in 1848 and at Cremorne Gardens, but evidence suggests that this design flew no better than its predecessor.

In France between 1856 and 1868 Captain Jean Marie le Bris attempted to fly a full-sized glider based on the shape of the albatross sea bird, and in about 1874 another French sailor, Felix du Temple, made a short hop in a powered monoplane after a ramp launch. Another notable French pioneer was Alphonse Pénaud, whose design for an amphibious two-seat tractor monoplane embodied many advanced features.

In 1884 the Russian Alexander Mozhaiski made a hop of 20–30 m (65–100 ft) after a take-off down a ramp, and the same year Britain's Horatio Phillips was granted his first patent for double-surface wing sections, which he had tested extensively in a wind tunnel. Phillips contributed greatly to the understanding of aerodynamics, and later tested some extraordinary aircraft incorporating a large number of 'slat' aerofoils in a 'Venetian blind' arrangement.

Above The German Otto Lilienthal pioneered the technique of hang gliding during the 1890s with monoplane and biplane machines, of which this one is typical.

Above right The classic braced biplane structure was introduced in the biplane hang glider, evolved by the naturalized American Octave Chanute in 1896.

The first powered aeroplane to raise itself from the ground was the ungainly *Eole* designed and built by Clement Ader, a French electrical engineer. Powered by an excellent 18–20 hp steam engine also designed by Ader, it covered 50 m (165 ft) on October 9, 1890. A successor, the *Avion III*, was tested on a circular track at Satory, near Versailles, on October 12 and 14, 1897, but failed to take to the air. In England a similar fate befell the enormous flying machine built at Baldwyn's Park, Kent, by the expatriate American Hiram Maxim. Spanning 31.79 m (104 ft) and powered by a pair of 180 hp steam engines, it was badly damaged during a test run on July 31, 1894. It fouled the restraining rails of the test track and the costly experiment was abandoned.

It was at this point that America began to rise to

the challenge, producing as a first champion the astronomer and mathematician Samuel Pierpoint Langley. Following prolonged experiments with models, wing sections and unsuccessful steam-driven designs, his fifth and sixth *Aerodrome* models made flights of 1005.8 m (3,300 ft) and 1.02 km (¾ mile) in 1896. Unfortunately the full-sized *Aerodrome A*, twice launched by catapult from the roof of a houseboat on the Potomac River in 1903, failed to fly on both occasions, probably suffering a structural failure on the second attempt.

Most of the aforementioned experimenters had attempted to fly without perfecting a means by which their large and cumbersome machines could be controlled. But there were also those who reasoned that it was no use taking off in a powered aeroplane unless one could control it once airborne, and who therefore decided to gain gliding experience first. The leading proponent of this belief was the German Otto Lilienthal, who, with his brother Gustav, had made numerous experiments with flapping wings while still at school.

In 1889, after an intensive study of bird flight, Lilienthal's findings were published in the book

Der Vogelflug als Grundlage der Fliegekunst ('Bird Flight as the basis of Aviation'). That year he built his first glider, followed by a second in 1890, and tested both of them at or near his home in Berlin-Lichterfelde. Although initially unsuccessful, he persevered and began to achieve promising results with his *No 6* of 1893. By 1894 he was flying his *No 9* machine from the Stöllner Hills, and the same year saw the appearance of his most successful glider, the *No 11*. All of Lilienthal's machines were hang gliders, with the pilot suspended in the framework between the wings and controlling his direction and speed by shifting his torso and legs from side to side and back and forth. More than eight No 11s were built for friends and customers, and Lilienthal achieved glides of up to 350 m (1,150 ft) in this type.

In 1895 Lilienthal built and flew three biplane gliders which, having less span than the monoplanes, proved easier to control. He also planned to fit a two-cylinder carbonic acid gas motor in a monoplane glider to power propulsive wingtip 'feathers', but no attempts at powered flight were made in that kind of machine.

Then, on August 9, 1896, Lilienthal was gliding in a No 11-type glider when it stalled and side-slipped to the ground. Lilienthal was badly hurt and died the following day. He had amassed a total of 2,500 gliding flights in five years, but his total time in the air amounted to only five hours, hardly enough to fully master the difficult control problem.

But he had not died in vain, for his work had been widely publicized all over the world, and his example was to fire the imagination of numerous disciples. In Britain the Scotsman Percy Pilcher built and flew four hang gliders between 1895 and 1899, culminating in the successful *Hawk,* first flown in 1896. He died when the tail of this glider collapsed in flight on September 30, 1899, just as he was about to install an engine in an untried triplane.

Around about 1855 Octave Chanute, a French-born civil engineer living in America, became interested in aeronautics and began to collect information on the subject. On retiring from full-time employment as a railway engineer in 1884 he devoted all his time to the cause, corresponding with more than 200 enthusiasts worldwide and writing a series of articles which in 1894 appeared in book form as the classic *Progress in Flying Machines.* This work was the first comprehensive historical study of the subject and quickly became the bible of the pioneers.

Chanute then embarked on a series of hang-glider experiments aimed at producing an automatic-stability system. Assisted by A. M. Herring, he began tests in 1896 with a multiplane which started life with six wings and ended up with four, in which form it made many glides. It was in this quadruplane that Chanute first used the civil engineers' Pratt Truss system to brace the wings, a method subsequently used on nearly all multi-winged aeroplanes.

Chanute's second glider made the greatest impact on the development of the aeroplane. Starting out as a triplane, it soon lost a plane and in this form was used for several hundred glides of between 45.7 m and 109.7 m (150 ft to 360 ft) in length. More important, it was also to provide the structural basis for the gliders built by the Wright Brothers.

Away from the mainstream of development, the experiments of Lawrence Hargrave of New South Wales, Australia, first came into prominence in 1885. His greatest contribution was the invention of the box-kite, on which many aeroplanes were later to be based. Hargrave's first full-sized aircraft

was a tandem-monoplane hang glider tested in 1894. This was followed by three designs for powered machines based on the box-kite, the last of which was built but failed to fly.

First flight at Kitty Hawk

It was the story of Otto Lilienthal's experiments that inspired Wilbur and Orville Wright, the sons of an American United Brethren Church bishop of Dayton, Ohio, to conduct their own aeronautical experiments. In May 1899 Wilbur wrote for information to the Smithsonian Institution, and by August of that year the brothers had built a biplane glider spanning 1.5 m (5 ft). Lateral control was achieved by twisting ('warping') the trailing edges of the wings, an idea which resulted directly from Wilbur's observations of birds.

Results were sufficiently encouraging to justify the production of a full-sized glider the following year. This was tested in October 1900 at Kitty

Hawk, North Carolina, a site which offered steady, strong winds and privacy. In 1901 a larger glider was flown as far as 112.56 m (389 ft), but the Wrights were not entirely satisfied with its performance. Suspecting that the data compiled by Lilienthal were at fault, they built their own wind tunnel and conducted extensive tests on model aerofoils from September 1901 to August 1902. The importance of this work cannot be exaggerated. Their thoroughness and fully professional, scientific approach was unprecedented in aeronautical history, and it laid the foundations for the achievements which followed.

The third glider, first flown on September 20, 1902, proved the soundness of their researches, making nearly 1,000 fully controlled glides by the end of October. The final control problem was solved by fitting a movable rudder which acted in concert with the wing warping. By then both brothers were skilful pilots, having flown up to 189.6 m (622½ ft) and having remained airborne for as long as 26 seconds.

Then, in the summer of 1903, the Wrights began to build a powered aeroplane. Like all their predecessors, they found that a suitably light and efficient powerplant was not to be had, a problem which they solved by designing and building their own 12 hp water-cooled internal-combustion engine. They also made their own airscrews at a time when the necessary technology was virtually non-existent. The magnitude of this achievement is best expressed by the fact that the propellers on their first powered aircraft, the *Flyer*, had an efficiency of 60 per cent, an enormous improvement on anything achieved up to that time.

The *Flyer* spanned 12.29 m (40 ft 4 in) and the engine drove the two pusher propellers through chain drives, one of which was crossed so that the propellers counter-rotated. Take-off was to be made along a 18.2 m (60 ft) launching rail, with the

aircraft riding on a small trolley until lift-off. A maiden flight was attempted unsuccessfully on December 14, 1903. Wilbur, lying prone in the hip cradle connected to the wing-warping mechanism, over-controlled with elevator and the machine ploughed into the sand. On 17 December the *Flyer* was again set up and Orville took off at 10.35 in the morning, making a 12-second flight and covering 36.5 m (120 ft). The first powered flight in history was followed by three more, the last covering 259 m (852 ft) in 59 seconds, or just over half a mile through the air allowing for the headwind. It culminated in a heavy landing which damaged the elevator and concluded the trials. For the first time man had made powered, sustained and controlled flights, although a fully practical aeroplane had still to be developed.

Testing of the 1904 *Flyer II* took place at the Huffman Prairie near Dayton. Some 80 brief flights were made, many featuring assisted take-offs: a weight linked to the aircraft by cable and pulleys was dropped from a derrick, accelerating the *Flyer II* along its rail. The first circular flight

was made during these trials, after which it became a common manoeuvre. Throughout this time the press took no notice of the Wright brothers' efforts and achievements, although there were many reports of the flights from local inhabitants. Many authorities were still insisting that powered flight was impossible.

The *Flyer III* of 1905 represented the first completely practical powered aeroplane in history. The Wrights logged more than three hours in the air during the 1905 season. Over 40 flights were made, the longest of which covered 38.94 km (24.2 miles) in 38 minutes 3 seconds on 5 October. This spectacular run of achievements was then halted when attempts to interest the US and some foreign governments failed, largely because the Wrights were reluctant to show their machine without first making a firm sale. Piqued, they suspended their experiments until 1908.

Europe takes up the challenge

While the Wrights had made enormous progress in the United States, Europe's pioneers were still

Far left One of the Wright gliders being tested. On the basis of their glider experiments the Wrights made the successful transition to powered flight in 1903.

Left An early aviator sits among the struts and braces of a biplane. The structure of these planes were of wood pinned or bolted together, braced with tight wires and covered with fabric.

Below left A rare original Blériot XI monoplane. This one is powered by a 25 hp Anzani engine and is similar to the type used by Blériot in his famous flight across the English Channel in 1909.

struggling to master basic principles. Their work lacked the patient, scientific approach of the Wrights, and their gliders, many of which were based on illustrations of Wright machines, were crude by comparison.

Despite attempts to follow the lead of the Wrights, it was not until October 1906 that any sort of powered flight was made in Europe. Even then, the best that Brazilian airship pioneer Santos Dumont could manage in his primitive canard biplane was 21.2 seconds. Four years after the Wrights' 59-second flight of 1903, Henri Farman made a marginally longer flight in a Voisin biplane. Then, on January 13, 1908, he made the first official, albeit inadequately controlled, circular flight in Europe. By August 1908, marginally controllable Voisin, Blériot and Antoinette monoplanes were able to stay up for only 20 minutes at a time.

That same month, the Europeans were shaken by the arrival of Wilbur Wright at Le Mans with the latest Wright biplane. For the first time they saw with their own eyes what a practical aeroplane flown by a competent pilot could do. The lesson was driven home, and within three years European aviation was to outpace even the Wrights. On October 30, 1908, Henri Farman made the world's first cross-country flight, covering 26.5 km (16½ miles). And on 16 October that year the first flight in Britain was made by the expatriate American S. F. Cody, who had already achieved some fame for his work on kites and airships. He covered 423.67 m (1,390 ft) in 27 seconds at Farnborough, Hants.

The year 1909 saw European aviation taking the first steps towards maturity, as evidenced by an event which vividly demonstrated the aeroplane's potential. On 25 July Louis Blériot flew his frail No XI monoplane, powered by a faltering three-cylinder 25 hp Anzani engine, across the Channel

Right The Antoinette monoplane was designed by Leon Levavasseur (1863–1922).

Below The Antoinette is here seen taking part in an early flying meeting.

16

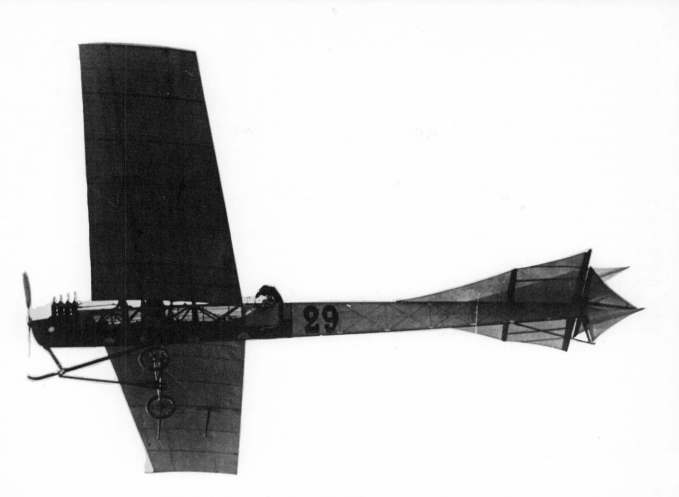

to land on top of the cliffs of Dover, spelling out the end of Britain's island security. In France the first great aviation meeting was held at Reims in August. Twenty-one aeroplanes took to the air and 87 flights exceeding 5 km (3 miles) were accomplished. The principal machines at Reims were the eminently practical Henri Farman, Wright, Curtiss and Voisin biplanes, and the Antoinette and Blériot XI monoplanes.

The abilities of some of the Reims machines were greatly enhanced by the appearance in 1907 of the 50 hp Gnome rotary engine, based on work by Laurent Seguin. In this engine the crankshaft remained fixed, and the seven cylinders, crankcase and propeller revolved around it. The cylinders thus cooled themselves, and the engine had a good power-to-weight ratio for its time. Rotary engines were to play a notable part in aviation until the 1920s.

The year 1910 witnessed a burgeoning of public interest in aviation, fostered by organised races, meetings and competitive flying. Successful copies of the leading designs were produced in every continent and flown on all manner of record-breaking flights. On 28 March the Frenchman Henri Fabre made the world's first seaplane flight in a curious Gnome-powered machine, and in April 1910 two Farman biplanes flown by Louis

Paulhan and England's Claude Grahame-White vied for the *Daily Mail's* £10,000 prize for the first London–Manchester flight. Despite a daring night flight by Graham-White, the prize was taken by the Frenchman. The Englishman consoled himself by winning the Gordon Bennett speed contest at America's international Belmont Park Meeting.

The Hon Charles Rolls made a double crossing of the Channel on 2 June in a Wright biplane, and in America Glenn Curtiss had evolved a highly successful biplane. It was one of these, piloted by Eugene Ely, which later took off from a platform on the foredeck of the US cruiser *Birmingham*. S. F. Cody, by then a naturalized British citizen, made a 298.5 km (185½-mile) flight lasting 4 hr 47 min in December to win the British Empire Michelin Cup. Geoffrey de Havilland, first of a great aircraft-manufacturing line, entered the scene with a successful Henri Farman-type biplane, following the failure of his first design. He was snatched up, aeroplane and all, as designer and test pilot of the British Government's aircraft factory at Farnborough. Originally called the Balloon Factory, it was renamed the Army Aircraft Factory in April.

Flying meetings proliferated in America and Britain and on the Continent, and aeroplane manufacturers were able to display their wares under cover at the Paris Salon and at Olympia in

London. Following the first, often unsuccessful attempts to open flying fields, aerodromes were established at Reims, Pau, Nice and Juvisy in France, and at Eastchurch, Brooklands and Hendon in England. Brooklands, already a famous motor-racing venue, became the aviator's Mecca, where new designs were evolved and tested. Hendon was the scene of many a pre-war weekend display attended by thousands of spectators.

That year the first woman pilot qualified. France's Baroness de Laroche trained on a Voisin and was awarded her certificate on 8 March. Regrettably the year also witnessed the passing of several great pioneers, including Britain's C. S. Rolls, who crashed on 12 July during the Bournemouth aviation meeting.

A notable 'first' went to Germany's Deutsche Luftschiffarts AG (DELAG), which inaugurated a passenger-carrying airship service between German cities. Between 1910 and 1914 DELAG's five Zeppelins were to carry more than 35,000 passengers without injury for a total distance of 273,588 km (170,000 miles).

Distance began to be conquered in 1911. Most notably, C. P. Rodgers flew his Wright EX biplane, named the *Vin Fiz* after a popular grape drink, from New York to Long Beach in a 6437.4 km (4,000-mile) flight lasting 49 days from September to November. By the time he reached his destination he had flown for 82 hours in 82 stages, and after 19 en route crashes little of his original aeroplane remained. Distance flying was encouraged in the form of races between great cities such as Paris and Rome, and by the first European Circuit Race. The latter was flown over some 1,000 miles from Paris through Brussels, London, Amiens and back to the starting point, and was won by a Lt Conneau flying under the pseudonym 'André Beaumont'.

Aeroplanes and engines were now becoming more sound and dependable, metal was increasingly being introduced into their structures, and well designed monoplanes and biplanes were coming from companies whose names were destined to become famous in the years ahead — Avro, Blériot, Blackburn, Bristol, Handley Page, Vickers, Nieuport and Hanriot.

From Farnborough in 1912 came the B.E.1 biplane, progenitor of another great design family, and in France the Maurice Farman Longhorn emerged, with its forward elevator on an enormous outrigger. This was the machine on which so many future pilots were destined to feel their way into the air for the first time. In San Diego Curtiss came up with the first practical seaplane when he attached a large central float to his standard pusher biplane, stabilizing it with small wingtip floats. It first flew in this form on 26 January.

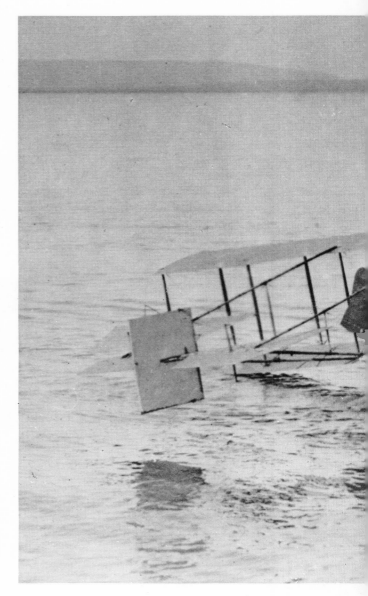

Aeroplanes for sport, business — and war

As the capabilities of aircraft expanded steadily, so they began to attract the attention of the military authorities, who quickly recognised the warlike potential of the flying machine. Britain and France both held military meetings, live bomb-dropping trials took place in the USA, and rifles and machine guns were taken into the air. Captain Piazza of Italy introduced the aeroplane to war when he flew his Blériot from Tripoli on a reconnaissance flight over Turkish positions near Azizia on 22 October. Airmail flying also began to make the news, although these first flights were only token efforts motivated mainly by a desire for publicity.

Perhaps the most noteworthy structural development of 1912 was the monocoque fuselage, in which all or most of the flying loads are taken by the fuselage skin rather than the internal framework. This technique was successfully employed in a beautifully streamlined Deperdussin

On February 17, 1911, Glenn Curtiss landed this seaplane near the USS *Pennsylvania* in San Diego harbour. The aircraft was hoisted aboard, then lowered to the water and flown back to base.

Left The Gnome-engined Sopwith Tabloid biplane first flew late in 1913 and had a top speed of 147 kmh (92 mph). A float-equipped variant captured the second Schneider Trophy Race for Great Britain in 1914.

his labours, but he could surely never have predicted the great strides destined to be made during the next half-century.

Most notable event of early 1913 was the maiden flight of Farnborough's B.S.1. This small aeroplane — designed by Geoffrey de Havilland and H. P. Folland, and powered by a 100 hp Gnome rotary giving a speed of 148.1 km/h (92 mph) — was the first single-seat scout aircraft in the world. Another product of the Royal Aircraft Factory, as it was called by then, was the inherently stable B.E.2 biplane, destined to serve in large numbers as a reconnaissance machine in the impending war.

From the spectators' point of view, 1913 was the year of aerobatics. Inverted flying and loops were performed by Adolphe Pégoud of France in September, although the Russian Nesterov had looped before him in late August, and 'stunts' soon became a regular feature of flying displays.

Speedy products from the private manufacturers included an even faster monocoque Deperdussin on which Prevost broke the world speed record no less than three times, reaching 203.1 km/h (126.7 mph) on the final attempt, and Sopwith's smart little Tabloid tractor biplane, which attained 148.1 km/h (92 mph) on the power of an 80 hp Gnome.

Destined for a great career was A. V. Roe's new 504 biplane. Several examples of a later variant, the 504N, would survive to see service in World War II. From Russia came news of the world's first four-engined aircraft, Igor Sikorsky's *Bolshoi* cabin biplane. Making its first flight on May 13, 1913, it was to sire the famous *Ilia Mourometz* bombers of the First World War.

Tragedy marred 1913 when Britain's pioneer S. F. Cody and a passenger, the cricketer W. H. B. Evans, were killed after Cody's aeroplane broke up in flight over Laffan's Plain, Farnborough.

One record which will now never be beaten fell to Noel Pemberton Billing on 17 September, when he won a £500 wager by learning to fly before breakfast — without any previous instruction whatsoever! More rationally, the first non-stop Mediterranean crossing, by Roland Garros in a Morane-Saulnier monoplane, testified to the improved reliability of aeroplanes.

With war preparations gathering momentum, 1914 saw few particularly notable achievements in aviation. But Sikorsky's first *Ilia Mourometz* carried 16 people in one flight on 11 February, and in June it flew 2,560 km (1,590 miles) on a return flight from St Petersburg to Kiev which included several stops and some night flying.

In America P. E. Fansler employed A. Jannus to pilot a Benoist flying boat on the first scheduled airline in history, operating between St Petersburg and Tampa, Florida. Several companies, including

monoplane which, powered by a 140 hp Gnome engine, won the Gordon Bennett Cup at Chicago on 9 September, at the same time capturing the world speed record at 173.9 km/h (108.2 mph).

Moving on from the seaplane, Curtiss then built his first successful flying boat. Monaco was the scene of the first seaplane meeting, attended by seven biplanes, in March 1912. More ominous however were the developments in the military sphere. In April Britain's Royal Flying Corps was founded, followed in August by a Military Aeroplane Competition on Salisbury Plain. The 30 aeroplanes entered were outperformed by de Havilland's B.E.2, which, as a Government aircraft, was not eligible for a prize. Ironically, the winner, Cody's large new biplane, was not regarded as a practical military machine and did not go into production.

Demonstrations underlining the areoplanes' naval potential were made by Lt C. R. Samson, who on 10 January took off on a Short pusher biplane from a wooden runway laid on the fore guns of HMS *Africa* while the ship was at anchor. This was followed later the same year by take-offs from HMS *Hibernia* and HMS *London* while they were under way, presaging the appearance of the aircraft carrier.

On 30 May Wilbur Wright died of typhoid fever at the age of 45. He had lived to see the first fruits of

Curtiss in America and Martinsyde and Handley Page in Britain, were confident enough to build large aeroplanes in an attempt to win Lord Northcliffe's £10,000 prize for the first non-stop transatlantic flight. But in the event war was to postpone this great conquest until 1919.

Howard Pixton kept the Sopwith Tabloid, now fitted with floats, in the limelight by flying it to first place in the second Schneider Trophy contest at an average speed of 141.4 km/h (87.8 mph), capping this with a new seaplane speed record of 148.1 km/h (92 mph). In Germany some of the most advanced designs were the big biplanes produced by the DFW company, while Pemberton Billing showed off the abilities of British manufacturers by designing, building and flying his little P.B.9 Scout within the space of nine days. By a dark coincidence, the drawings for it were dated August 4, 1914 — the day Britain declared war on Germany.

Above left Henri Farman (1874–1958) standing in front of his Voisin-Farman No 1 biplane. In this plane Farman flew, on 13 January 1908, the first one-kilometre circuit in Europe.

Top Typical of many boxkite biplanes was the Bristol Boxkite of 1910. *The Phoenix Flyer,* illustrated here, is a replica specially made for the film *Those Magnificent Men in their Flying Machines.*

Above The first indigenous aeroplane to fly in Switzerland was the Dufax biplane, which was flown across Lake Geneva on August 28, 1919. It is now preserved in a museum.

Chapter 2
WORLD WAR I

I N the decade between Kitty Hawk and the outbreak of the Great War, the aeroplane had been refined from an airborne curiosity into a fairly reliable vehicle which, given a little luck, could do what was expected of it. The infant air arms of the warring nations had ideas of using their aircraft for artillery spotting or reconnaissance, but, officially at least, not for combat. None of them carried military equipment of any kind, let alone weapons. Yet under the stimulus of the most savage war in human history, the aircraft was to be transformed into an efficient air-to-air and air-to-surface killing machine capable of outdoing its pre-war ancestors in every area of performance, often by factors of two, three or four. If nothing else, World War I was to lay the foundations for the 20 years of steady progress in aviation which followed the Armistice.

The war spread to most of the nations of Europe in the last days of July and the first days of August

The French Morane-Saulnier Type N, mounting a single gun. It was, however, primarily used for observation flights.

1914. Few men at first saw how different this war was to be compared with earlier European conflicts, and the general consensus was that it would be short and sharp. Consequently, little or nothing had been done to prepare for a long conflict.

This is particularly evident in the use of 'air power' in the early months of the war. There were about 390 aircraft available to the combatants in the Western theatre of operations at the outbreak of hostilities (136 French, 48 British and 24 Belgian against about 180 German machines); but these were a hotch-potch of different designs that could hardly be grouped into homogeneous squadrons. The British were in the worst position, flying a motley of B.E.2 variants, Avro 504s, Sopwith Tabloids and Bristol Scouts, plus a few French-designed machines. The French were slightly better off, being equipped with Morane-Saulniers of various types, Caudron G.IIIs, and a number of large Voisins which were pressed into service as rudimentary bombers. The Germans were equipped with a large quantity of Taube types and Albatros B.Is and B.IIs.

With some notable exceptions, such as the Sopwith Tabloid and the Morane-Saulnier Type N, most of these machines had a maximum speed of about 121 km/h (75 mph) and an endurance of some three hours. Armament was officially forbidden by most authorities, and it was only the most enterprising of pilots who took a pistol or carbine with him. Moreover, as a result of the almost total lack of government preparation in the last years of peace, these aircraft were intrinsically civilian types little able to undertake military tasks — the most important of which was to observe the enemy's movements behind his lines.

Above The Sopwith Snipe, a single-seat fighter produced in 1919. Fast and reliable, it became the RAF's standard fighter for several years.

Above right The Fokker D VII, regarded as one of the best fighter-scout aircraft produced during World War I in any country.

Right The Morane-Saulnier Parasol, a reconnaissance aircraft which evolved during World War I into one of the first fighters.

The best types for reconnaissance in the early months of the war were the French Morane-Saulnier parasols and the pusher Farmans. The Morane-Saulnier Type L clearly reflected that firm's design preferences: the wing was mounted above the fuselage on a framework of struts supported by bracing wires. The crew, sitting underneath the wing, had an almost uninterrupted downward view. A different philosophy was apparent in such designs as the Farman M.F.7 and 11. Here the layout was based on the pusher principle, with the engine mounted behind the wings and driving a pusher propeller. The tail structure was mounted on booms stretching back from the wings outside the disc swept by the propeller. Naturally enough, little in the way of slipstreaming could be achieved with such a design, and performance was

lower than that of tractor types. But, more importantly perhaps in those early days, the crew was accommodated in a shoe-like nacelle perched on the leading edge of the wing. This afforded both the pilot and the observer an excellent view forward and downward.

It was with such equipment that the airmen of World War I started their eventful careers; not surprisingly, a dread of mechanical failure on the part of their own aircraft was a far more dominant factor than any fear of enemy action. Even though many pilots ignored official policy and attempted to arm their aircraft, they were almost universally unsuccessful in providing themselves with effective weapons. The first months of the war were marked by an amazing assortment of supposedly lethal gadgets fitted to aircraft: there were guns firing at 45° to the line of flight in order to clear the propeller (which made sighting all but impossible); boxes of steel darts; some crews even carried grappling hooks or bricks fixed on the end of a length of line, with which they tried to break off enemy propellers.

Probably the most important single contribution made by aircraft in 1914 was the news brought by the crew of a British machine that the German right flank, which was intended to sweep round the west side of Paris early in September, had in fact veered more to the south and would now pass to the east of the French capital. This opened the eyes of the Allied High Command to the possibility of a counterstroke from Paris as the German flank moved past. The result was the Battle of the Marne, Germany's first serious setback in World War I.

As yet there were no true fighting aircraft. The machines described above were merely short-term expedients. The problem which held up further development is simple to describe: the machines with the highest performances, and therefore the best chance of catching an opponent and forcing him down, were the tractor-engined biplane scouts such as the Bristol Scout or Avro 504. But because they had a propeller in front of the pilot, it was impossible to mount a machine-gun on the fusel-age in such a way that it could fire forward through the disc swept by the propeller.

The first fighters

A machine was then produced that can be considered as the world's first true fighting aeroplane. This was the Vickers F.B.5, nicknamed the 'Gunbus', which had been designed from the outset for aerial combat on the principle that if it was worth getting one's own air reconnaissance, it was also worth preventing the other side getting theirs. The Vickers F.B.5 was a conventional two-seat pusher biplane, in which the pilot sat in the rear seat and the gunner/observer in the front seat, from which he commanded an excellent field of fire and observation. Armament was a single 0.303 in Lewis gun. The chief fault of the F.B.5 (Fighting

Left and below This aircraft, the Sopwith Pup, was used by the Royal Naval Air Service to develop the concept of aircraft carriers. It came into service in 1916 and became one of the most popular fighters used by the Royal Flying Corps.

Top The Vickers F.B.5 'Gunbus'; the observer/gunner sat in front of the pilot, where he had an excellent view and field of fire.

Above The Fokker Eindekker was the first aircraft to be supplied with the interrupter gear which enabled the pilot to fire through the propeller.

Above right Typical of the more advanced fighter aircraft of 1917 was the French Spad 13, many of which were flown by the U.S. Air Service.

Biplane) was that it was a pusher, with all that basic type's failings in terms of performance (speed 113 km/h [70 mph] and ceiling 9,000 ft). The type began to arrive in France in February 1915.

The next step in the evolution of the fighter aeroplane was crucial but also, paradoxically, quite false. Early in 1914, Raymond Saulnier of the Morane-Saulnier company had seen where the true answer to air combat lay: in the production of a gun that fired along the line of sight and line of flight of pilot and aeroplane. But the propeller of any tractor type would be in the way, so how was he to overcome this problem? Clearly it was necessary to halt the stream of bullets from the machine-gun whenever a propeller blade was in the line of fire; this could be done, Saulnier saw, by synchronizing the action of the machine-gun with the movement of the propeller. Saulnier designed an interrupter gear that would achieve this, but the uncertain quality of French machine-gun ammunition was

such that rounds might 'hang fire' and then go off when the next blade was in the line of fire. To mitigate the effects of such stray rounds on the wooden propeller blade, Saulnier fitted wedge-shaped steel deflectors to the rear of each blade, along the line of fire. The problem of the ammunition appeared impossible, however, and Saulnier abandoned his experiments.

In the spring of 1915, French pre-war stunt pilot and aviation pioneer Roland Garros was serving with the French Air Force. Disgruntled by his lack of success in shooting down German reconnaissance machines, Garros persuaded Saulnier to let him use the Type L parasol monoplane fitted with the deflectors only, the interrupter gear having been removed. In less than three weeks Garros had disposed of five German reconnaissance machines. But then on 10 April his luck changed, and he was forced down behind the German lines and captured, together with his machine.

The Germans at once realized the significance of the deflectors and decided to develop an efficient system for their own aircraft. A young Dutch designer working in Germany, Anthony Fokker, was called in and told to produce a proper interrupter gear. A few days later the result was ready for testing, and proved entirely successful. Fokker persuaded the German authorities to allow him to test the new interrupter in one of his own aircraft, an M5K monoplane, and, when the air tests proved equally successful, to order from him fighter aircraft using this device. The result was the Fokker E.I monoplane, the world's first true single-seat fighter. In all ways an indifferent machine, indeed a dangerous one, the E.I nearly always prevailed by virtue of its superior armament — a synchronized 7.92 mm Parabellum machine-gun.

In the hands of pilots such as Oswald Boelcke and Max Immelmann, the Fokker proved itself

Above For aircraft like the Avro 504K biplane powered by engines of 100 to 130 hp, hand-swinging was the only means available for starting the engine.

Above right For the more powerful engine of the F.2A/F.2B Bristol Fighter, a mobile Huck's Starter was used. Its engine was connected to the propeller by a metal shaft.

Right The Curtiss JN-4, used as a primary trainer until 1927. These aircraft were also the main mount of the first barnstormers, the men who popularized flying throughout the U.S.A.

master of the skies over the Western Front, so much so that the period from autumn 1915 to spring 1916 is now known in aviation history as the time of the 'Fokker scourge'.

Lacking an interrupter gear of their own, the French and British had to find other, short-term solutions while development went on. The first answer was the French Nieuport 11 or 'Bébé'. This was a compact, high-performance machine armed with a Lewis gun on the upper wing which fired over the propeller. Considerably faster, more manoeuvrable and stronger than the Fokker, the Nieuport 11 began the eclipse of the German type.

The Nieuport was soon joined in this task by Britain's answer, the de Havilland D.H.2. This was introduced in the spring of 1916 and was issued to No 24 Squadron, which thus became the first British squadron to be equipped throughout with single-seat fighters. The D.H.2 was a small pusher biplane with the Lewis gun mounted in the nose. With the large-scale arrival of D.H.2s in France the Fokker was totally outclassed and the Allies

enjoyed a period of complete air supremacy. The other major fighting aeroplane of the day was the Royal Aircraft Factory's F.E.2b, a big and sturdy two-seat pusher biplane that was used for escort, bombing and reconnaissance missions.

Eyes in the sky
While the development of fighter aircraft had been progressing, the main burden of air operations rested on the shoulders of the crews of the various types of reconnaissance and artillery-spotting machines shuttling up and down the front. It was the protection or destruction of these all-important types that was the *raison d'être* of the new fighters.

The British were still using large numbers of the inherently stable B.E.2s, but a new type, the R.E.8, began to enter service in the second half of 1916. The R.E.8 acquired an unenviable and not altogether justified reputation as a tricky aircraft to fly, but fulfilled its tasks excellently in the last two years of the war. It had a top speed of 164 km/h (102 mph), an endurance of 4¼ hours and an armament

of one fixed 0.303 in Vickers machine-gun, firing through the disc swept by the propeller with the aid of the newly developed British interrupter gear, and one (later two) Lewis guns for the observer. Another mainstay of the Royal Flying Corps and Royal Naval Air Service was the Sopwith 1½-Strutter, a delightful machine to fly and one that was capable of fulfilling the fighter, bomber and reconnaissance roles. It was the first British aircraft to be designed with provision for an interrupter gear. Capable of 171 km/h (106 mph), it could climb to 15,000 ft, had an endurance of 4½ hours and could carry up to 59 kg (130 lb) of bombs.

In the French Air Force, reconnaissance was still carried out by the types that had been in service since the early days of the war — Farmans, Caudrons, and Morane-Saulnier Types LA and P. The last type, introduced in 1915, had a speed of 156 km/h (97 mph), a ceiling of 12,000 ft, an endurance of 2½ hours and an armament of one fixed Vickers machine-gun and one flexible Lewis gun.

The Germans, on the other hand, had decided that their reconnaissance aircraft should be more capable of defending themselves without a fighter escort than were the Allied machines. The result was a series of startlingly efficient biplanes. Albatros, a firm that was later to become famous for its shark-like fighters, introduced the C III in 1916. With a top speed of 140 km/h (87 mph), the C III was not very fast, but it had good range, adequate

armament and was very sturdy. The type was supplanted later in 1916 by the C VII: this had a 200 hp instead of a 160 hp engine, which raised the top speed to 171 km/h (106 mph).

The year 1917 saw the introduction of some of the best German reconnaissance machines of the war. Albatros developed the C X and C XII, strong and fast machines that were built in substantial numbers. In that year also came the widespread entry into service of the DFW C V, developed late in 1916 from the earlier C IV. The C V was powered by the 200 hp Benz BzIV inline engine and had a top speed of 156 km/h (97 mph). With a ceiling of 16,400 ft and an endurance of 3½ hours, it was one of Germany's best all-round aircraft.

Infantry contact patrols were started in 1916 because commanders had been finding it impossible to establish where exactly their front-line troops had got to in offensives. Aircraft were thus sent out to find the markers which their troops had been ordered to lay out. The LVG C V, designed by the same man as the DFW C V, had a generally similar performance. The Rumpler C IV and C VII both appeared in 1917 and did excellent work for the Germans. These were basically similar to other German reconnaissance types, but in addition they both had a very good high-altitude performance, which made them relatively immune from the attentions of Allied fighters.

In 1917, too, came the introduction of the best all-round aeroplane of the war, the Bristol F.2

Left The Fokker Dr I triplane. The notorious 'Red Baron' was one of the many German pilots to fly this plane.

Below The Sopwith triplane. Its great success inspired the design of the German Fokker triplane.

Fighter. A very strong, handy design, with the fuselage suspended between the wings, the Bristol Fighter had an inauspicious entry into service because its pilots tried to adopt normal two-seater defensive tactics. But once they recognized the machine's potential for offensive work, with the observer covering the tail, the F.2A and its better development, the F.2B, became the war's best two-seaters.

Air combat: the shifting balance

While this advance in two-seaters was taking place, the balance of air supremacy was again shifting to the Germans. The Allies had capped their defeat of the Fokker monoplane in early 1916 by introducing during the summer the Sopwith Pup fighter. This was essentially a single-seat scaled-down version of the 1½-Strutter, and is generally recognized as the most perfect flying machine of World War I; with an engine of only 80 hp it was capable of 179 km/h (111 mph) and had a ceiling of 17,500 ft, at which altitude it was still highly manoeuvrable. But armament remained unchanged at one Vickers machine-gun. In the Allied squadrons the Pup was complemented by the Nieuport company's successor to the Bébé, the Nieuport 17. This had a single synchronized Vickers machine-gun and a performance very similar to the Pup's, but with a 110 hp rotary engine.

Of a different design philosophy was the French Spad S.7 fighter. This was a heavier and more powerful machine, still armed only with a single machine-gun, but capable of 192 km/h (119 mph) and a ceiling of 18,000 ft on the 175 hp of its Hispano-Suiza inline engine. Deliveries began in August 1916.

The Germans, however, had gone a step further in the evolution of the fighter when they introduced the Albatros D I and II fighters in the autumn and winter of 1916. Powered by a 160 hp Mercedes engine, the D II had a speed of 175 km/h (109 mph) at a ceiling of 17,060 ft. But whereas Allied fighters still had only one gun, the Albatros had two, which gave it a distinct advantage in firepower. The

PRM 735.

Germans followed up this advantage quickly, introducing the Albatros D III in the spring of 1917. This was an updated D II, with wings of greater span supported by V-shaped interplane struts instead of the earlier models' parallel struts. With the arrival of the D III German supremacy was complete, and the immediate result was 'Bloody April' 1917, when Allied types, mostly British, were shot down in droves.

German supremacy did not last long, however. In spring 1917 the first of the Royal Aircraft Factory's new fighter, the S.E.5 arrived in France, followed in early summer by its higher-powered development, the S.E.5a. The latter was powered by a 200 hp Wolseley Viper engine in its definitive version, compared with the S.E.5's 150 hp Hispano-Suiza. Both were armed with a synchronized Vickers machine-gun in the fuselage and a Lewis gun firing over the propeller arc on the upper wing. The S.E.5a had a top speed of 222 km/h (138 mph) and a ceiling of 19,500 ft, with an excellent rate of climb as well.

At about the same time that the first S.E.5as were reaching the squadrons, another new British fighter was making its appearance. This was the redoubtable Sopwith F.I Camel, the war's most successful fighter (in terms of aircraft destroyed). The Camel was designed as a successor to the Pup.

Although it had a slightly greater span than its predecessor, the Camel had a shorter fuselage. In the forward seven feet of this were crammed the pilot, fuel, guns and ammunition, and a 100-170 hp rotary engine. With most of the aeroplane's weight close to the centre of gravity, the Camel had phenomenal agility, though it took an experienced pilot to make the most of it. With a 130 hp Clerget rotary, top speed was 185 km/h (115 mph) and ceiling 19,000 ft.

Earlier in the year, in an effort to improve the pilot's view and increase the rate of climb — without losing any of the Pup's manoeuvrability — the Sopwith company had produced the Sopwith Triplane for the RNAS. This featured three narrow-chord staggered wings braced only by two plank-type interplane struts. The machine had a short and spectacular career until it was replaced by the Camel.

Just as the Camel had succeeded the Pup, in the French Air Force the Spad S.13 succeeded the Spad S.7 in the early summer of 1917. Armed with two machine-guns and equipped with a more powerful 235 hp Hispano-Suiza inline engine, the Spad S.13 also had aerodynamic refinements intended to improve manoeuvrability. Like the S.E.5a, it had a top speed of 222 km/h (138 mph), but it had a better ceiling (21,800 ft) and proved capable of taking on the latest German fighters up to the end of the war.

Spurred on by these Allied successes, the Germans also continued to improve their fighters. The Albatros works produced another version of their basic fighter design in the summer of 1917. This was the D V, powered by a 180 hp Mercedes inline. Basically similar to the D III, the D V was not much of an improvement on the earlier type, having a speed of 187 km/h (116 mph) and a ceiling of 20,500 ft. Essentially, the problem was that the design had reached its development limit; what was needed was another design.

The first new design to be produced in any quantity was the Fokker Dr I. This was a diminutive triplane inspired by the Sopwith Triplane. A top speed of 166 km/h (103 mph) made it slow compared with contemporary Allied designs, but its ceiling and rate of climb were good and its manoeuvrability excellent.

The right answer was not in fact found until 1918, when the Fokker D VII made its appearance. This design entered service in April 1918. It was powered by a 185 hp BMW inline engine and had a top speed of 200 km/h (124 mph) and a ceiling of 22,900 ft. But though its performance was only about the same as that of Allied fighters, its handling qualities at altitude, and its ability to 'hang' on its propeller, made it a formidable fighter. Fokker's last fighter of the war, the D VIII, is also worthy of note. This was a parasol-winged machine, powered by a rotary and not very fast, but agile with good rates of climb and dive.

In the Allied camp, a new generation of fighters would have entered the lists in large numbers if the war had continued into 1919, and some of these should be mentioned. Sopwith had just introduced two good designs: the Snipe fighter, a faster development of the Camel (which had been the first aircraft to fly from barges towed behind destroyers), and the Dolphin escort and ground-attack fighter. Another manufacturer, Martin & Handasyde, was about to commence large-scale delivery of the fastest Allied fighter to appear during the war, the F.4 Buzzard, which was powered by a 300 hp Hispano-Suiza inline and had a top speed of 233 km/h (145 mph).

Giant bombers and ground-attackers

Although the fighters were best-known to the public, and made the greatest advances in performance, there were other types of aircraft operating over the front that proved the real workhorses of the war. Whereas the early years from 1914 had seen little distinction in types other than into fighter and reconnaissance/bomber categories, in 1917 and 1918 the non-fighter types rapidly multiplied.

The British produced a pure bomber type, the D.H.4, which made its appearance in 1917. Essentially a light bomber, it was followed in 1918 by the D.H.9. The former was one of the best aircraft of the war, serving in large numbers with the British and Americans. With the 375 hp Rolls-Royce Eagle inline, the D.H.4 had a top speed of 230 km/h (143 mph), a ceiling of 22,000 ft and a range of 700 km (435 miles). Its defensive armament included up to four machine-guns, and its offensive load comprised 209 kg (460 lb) of bombs. The D.H.9 was intended as an improvement on the D.H.4, but its engine power was considerably less and performance suffered accordingly.

Right A squadron line-up of Royal Aircraft Factory S.E.5a's. These were outstanding single-seat fighters of World War I.

Below The German Albatros DIII, introduced in spring 1917. This was an updated DII, with interplane wing struts instead of the parallel type.

The first British version of what was intended to be a strategic bomber was the Handley-Page 0/100, which entered service in September 1916. Powered by two Rolls-Royce Eagle inlines of 250 hp each, the 0/100 had a speed of 137 km/h (85 mph) and a range of 1,127 km (700 miles). Defensive armament comprised three to five Lewis guns, and an offensive load was carried of up to 907 kg (2,000 lb) of bombs or a single 1,650-pounder. In 1918 Handley Page introduced an improved version of the 0/100, the 0/400. This was powered by two Rolls-Royce Eagles of 360 hp each, and had a speed of 157 km/h (97½ mph) and a range of 1,200 km (750 miles). Defensive armament included up to five Lewis guns, and the offensive load was again up to 2,000 lb of bombs. The largest British bomber of the war was the Handley-Page V/1500. Only six had been built by the time of the Armistice. Power was provided by four Rolls-Royce Eagles developing 375 hp each. This gave the bomber a speed of 156 km/h (97 mph) and a range of 1,932 km (1,200 miles). Armament was up to five Lewis guns and 3,400 kg (7,500 lb) of bombs.

In the French camp, one of the best aircraft of the war was produced in 1918. This was the Salmson 2A2, a reconnaissance type. Powered by a Salmson-Canton Unné water-cooled radial of 260 hp, the 2A2 had a top speed of 185 km/h (115 mph) and a ceiling of 20,500 ft. It was a very strong machine, and agile for its size. Its defensive armament of one fixed Vickers and two flexible Lewis guns enabled it to give a very good account of itself in combat.

France had become attached to the idea of bombing far sooner than the British, and by 1918 she had a large number of bomber squadrons. The types most commonly used by these units were the Breguet 14 and the Voisin Types 6 to 10. The Voisins had been in service since 1916. The Type 10 was powered by a 300 hp Renault inline driving a pusher propeller, and had a top speed of 135 km/h (84 mph) and a range of 500 km (310 miles). Bomb load was up to 272 kg (600 lb). The Breguet 14 was a far superior machine, and appeared in two versions, the 14A2 and the 14B2. The former was a two-seater reconnaissance machine, and the latter a bomber. Powered by a 300 hp Renault inline, the Breguet 14B2 was a large tractor biplane capable of 195 km/h (121 mph), a ceiling of 19,000 ft and a range of 530 km (330 mph). Armament comprised one fixed Vickers and two or three flexible Lewis guns, plus up to 236 kg (520 lb) of bombs.

The chief American contribution to the technical side of the air war lay in the field of engines. A large range of Liberty inlines was designed which, if the war had lasted into 1919, would have powered numerous types of Allied aircraft. The USA's own aircraft industry produced no worthwhile combat types of its own design during the war, with the exception of the Curtiss America series of flying boats.

Below One of the standard German bombers from 1917 onwards, the Gotha G V, a large though comparatively slow biplane.

Above right The Handley Page 0/400, a large twin-engined bomber introduced in 1918 with a much greater range than previous models.

By 1918 the Germans had produced a considerable number of aircraft types designed for bombing or ground attack. The standard German bombers from 1917 onwards were the Gotha G IV and G V. These were large tractor biplanes, and from the spring of 1917 onwards the former took over from the Zeppelins the task of bombing Great Britain. Power was provided by two 260 hp Mercedes inlines, and although speed was not spectacular at 140 km/h (87 mph), ceiling and range, at 21,320 ft and 490 km (305 miles), were more impressive. The G IV carried a bomb load of 500 kg (1,100 lb) and was protected by two flexible Parabellum machine-guns. However, in 1917–18 Germany produced some true giants. The most successful of these was the Zeppelin-Staaken R VI. This had a wingspan of 42 m (138.5 ft), (larger than the span of the Boeing B-17 Flying Fortress), and was powered by four 260 hp Mercedes inlines. Top speed was not good at 130 km/h (81 mph), but its endurance capability of 10 hours and bomb load of 1,800 kg (nearly 4,000 lb) were considerable.

In the field of ground-attack aircraft, Germany produced some most interesting designs. One of the earliest of these was the Halberstadt CL II, a two-seat tractor-engined biplane that appeared in 1917 and was soon supplemented by the improved CL IV. Armament was three machine-guns and the type proved very effective.

One of the early pioneers of all-metal construction for aircraft was Dr Hugo Junkers, whose armoured J I ground-attack machine appeared in the early summer of 1917. The J I was a large two-seat tractor biplane with thick-section cantilever wings. Its 200 hp Benz inline engine was not really enough for its considerable weight and size, and top speed was only 155 km/h (96 mph). But the armament of two fixed and one flexible machine-guns was good. Better than the J I, however, was the Junkers CL I of 1918. This was developed from the all-metal D I fighter, and was in effect a scaled-up version that took a crew of two. This handy, low-winged monoplane was immensely strong and would have played an important part if the war had continued into 1919.

Naval aircraft

The aircraft used in the early days of World War I for operations over the sea were of simple design and were intended merely to scout for signs of

The Handley Page V/1500, which was intended to carry out bombing raids on Berlin. However, the war ended before these got under way.

enemy activity. For this both landplanes and floatplanes were employed, and of the latter type the Sopwith Schneider and Baby were typical. Single-seat tractor biplanes, they were little more than landplanes adapted for sea use with the addition of twin floats. The British continued to use them throughout the war for scouting and anti-Zeppelin operations.

Far more importance was attached to the floatplane by the Central Powers. In Germany the main producers of floatplanes were Friedrichshafen and Hansa-Brandenburg, which also supplied most of Austria-Hungary's machines. Friedrichshafen's most successful floatplane was the FF 33, which first appeared in 1915 and was built in a bewildering number of variants for patrol and escort duties. The FF 33l, of autumn 1916, was powered by a 150 hp Benz inline. Apart from its twin floats, it was a perfectly conventional tractor biplane with a speed of 137 km/h (85 mph), an endurance of six hours

and an armament of one fixed and one flexible machine-gun.

Hansa-Brandenburg produced several very striking floatplane fighter and patrol aircraft under the design leadership of Ernst Heinkel. First came the KDW, whose biplane wings were braced with a star-shaped set of interplane struts. The type was mounted on twin floats and had a top speed of 172 km/h (107 mph) with its 160 hp Maybach inline engine, and was armed with two fixed machine-guns. The type was introduced in mid-1916 and was replaced a year later by the W 12 two-seater floatplane. Powered by a 150 hp Benz inline, the W 12 had a top speed of 161 km/h (100 mph) and was armed with three machine-guns. Heinkel's best design was the W 29, which appeared in mid-1918. This was a twin-seat twin-float monoplane, which could achieve 175 km/h (109 mph) on the 150 hp of its Benz inline.

Mention has already been made of the Curtiss flying boats, and from these were developed the best flying boats of the war, the British Porte-Felixstowe F.2A and F.3. The main failing of the Curtiss boats was the poor design of their hulls, and

so the new aircraft's designer, Squadron Commander J. C. Porte of the Royal Naval Air Service, worked out a new hull shape and fitted more powerful engines. The result was a handsome-looking and very efficient and formidable anti-submarine and patrol boat. The F.2A was powered by two Rolls-Royce Eagles of 345 hp each, which gave it a speed of 153 km/h (95 mph) and endurance of six hours; it was armed with seven Lewis guns and 209 kg (460 lb) of bombs. The type entered service in 1917.

Most important of all in the long term, however, was the introduction of shipborne aircraft. We have already seen that the first experiments were undertaken by the Americans, but the first landing on a moving ship was made by a British pilot in a Sopwith Pup on August 2, 1917. The British developed flying-off platforms on the turrets of capital ships and cruisers, but as there was no way of landing the reconnaissance aircraft back on the ship, the pilot had to ditch, which almost inevitably meant the loss of his machine. The British therefore began to conduct experiments with aircraft-carriers, the first of which, HMS *Furious*,

made possible the historic landing mentioned earlier. Thereafter much ingenuity was devoted to producing aircraft that could land on the early carriers on skids which reduced their landing runs. By the end of the war the *Furious* had been converted from its early form, with a taking-off platform in the bows and a landing-on platform in the stern, to a single full-length flying-deck from which ordinary wheeled aircraft could operate.

In reviewing the aircraft of World War I, two outstanding conclusions can be drawn. Firstly, enormous strides had been made in developing the aeroplane as a reliable, multi-purpose weapon. Engineers and aerodynamicists had produced sturdy machines that could stand up to combat conditions, and theorists had decided the roles that specific types of aircraft were to play. But one's second conclusion must be that the military use of aeroplanes was still in its infancy, and that the theorists had overreached themselves during the war, and would continue to do so after 1918. It was in fact to be many years before air forces would be able to act as a decisive arm, rather than as a lesser adjunct to forces on the ground.

Chapter 3
INTER-WAR YEARS

AT eleven o'clock on the morning of November 11, 1918, World War I officially ended. Four years of slaughter and utter waste were over, and it was time to draw breath before plunging into the arduous business of restoration. It was to be a long and difficult process. There were shortages of food, materials, housing, and in only one thing was Europe rich — war material. But what use was it, except as scrap?

Out of this mass of redundant equipment only the bomber aeroplane seemed to have any immediate practical purpose, especially in those regions where the roads and railways had been destroyed. For the time being, then, these aircraft could be pressed into service as transports.

Only 15 years had passed since the Wright Brothers had achieved the world's first powered and controlled flight, and for 11 of those years the aeroplane had improved very little. Then, spurred on by a desperate need to build aircraft bigger,

The Short Calcutta flying boat, used on part of the air-route to India. It could carry about 15 passengers at a maximum speed of 176 km/h (110 mph).

faster and more lethal than those of their enemies, the governments of the West invested so much in aircraft development that the years between 1914 and 1918 saw a revolution in aeroplane performance and design.

By the end of World War I, the Royal Air Force had grown from some 160 aircraft to a massive 22,647, and its strength in officers and men from 2,000 to nearly 300,000. Throughout Europe, hundreds of bombers, fighters and general-purpose types were standing idle on airfields. There were also the men, most of whom knew no other business than that of flying and servicing flying machines. The time was ripe for the enthusiasts and would-be pioneers to come forward and open up the world with the heavier-than-air machine.

Swords into ploughshares

The first post-war machine to attract the world's attention was a four-engined Handley Page V/1500

spanning 38.4 m (126 ft) and capable of a top speed of 166 km/h (103 mph). Piloted by Squadron Leader A. C. S. MacLaren and Lieutenant R. Bailey, and carrying a single passenger, it took off for India on December 13, 1918, reaching the subcontinent just over a month later. Although this historic flight seemed to attract little official interest, its effect on other pilots was galvanic.

One of the first countries to show real enthusiasm for this new mode of travel was Australia. In the spring of 1919 the Australian Government offered a prize of A£10,000 to any of its citizens who flew home from the UK in a British machine. This offer induced Ross Smith and his brother Keith to set off from Hounslow Airport in appalling weather on November 12, 1919, in a modified Vickers Vimy bomber. It was powered by

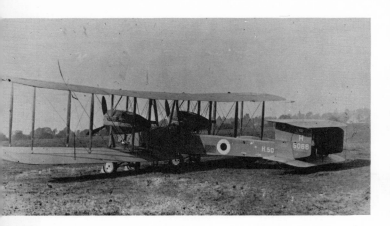

engine. In this he flew from London to Rangoon and back in 1924, and then from London to Cape Town and back in 1925. The following year, its wheels replaced by floats, the same machine flew to Australia and back.

By then people were seeing air travel in a new light, especially after the Australian Bert Hinkler showed the world what could be done in a light aeroplane well within the reach of many pockets. He had already flown non-stop from London to Turin in 1920, piloting an Avro Baby biplane with a Green 35 hp engine. Eight years later, in an Avro Avian powered by a 35 hp ADC Cirrus II, he made the first solo flight from England to Australia — some 17,700 km (11,000 miles) in 15½ days. In 1929 he flew a D.H.80A Puss Moth — a two/three-seat monoplane powered by a 120 hp de Havilland Gipsy III — from New York to London, making the first non-stop flight between New York and Jamaica. Such flights, graphically demonstrating the rugged reliability of the aircraft of the time, did more to sell aviation to the travelling public than all the expensive advertising in the world.

But of all the routes that beckoned to these post-war pioneers, the most enticing was Europe-America, across the North Atlantic. As early as 1913, when there existed no aircraft capable of such a journey, the London *Daily Mail* had offered a prize of £10,000 for the first non-stop flight between North America and Europe. Come the end of the war there were many long-range machines but the first men who set out to fly the Atlantic in 1919 were not competing for this prize. On 16 May three Navy-Curtiss flying boats, NC-1, NC-3 and NC-4, left Trepassey Bay in Newfoundland and headed for the Azores, 2,208 km (1,380 miles) away. Powered by four 400 hp Liberty 12 engines, these aircraft spanned 38.4 m (126 ft) and had a maximum speed of 146 km/h (91 mph). They had a range of 800 km (500 miles) but only one of them, Lieutenant-Commander Read's NC-4, completed this first leg. NC-4 went on to make history when it touched down in Plymouth Sound on 31 May to become the first heavier-than-air machine to fly the Atlantic.

The first pilot to try for the *Daily Mail* prize was Henry Hawker, flying a Sopwith biplane powered by a 375 hp 12-cylinder Rolls-Royce engine.

two 360 hp Rolls-Royce Eagle VIII twelve-cylinder engines each driving a four-bladed propeller 3.20 m (10½ ft) in diameter. Again, its maximum speed was about 166 km/h. The Smiths flew through storms over Europe and battled a monsoon from Rangoon to Bangkok. Then, at Surabaya, they found the aerodrome flooded and had to call for tons of bamboo matting to be laid down to provide a runway. In spite of all this, they touched down at Darwin on 10 December after 188 hours in the air.

Another early challenge was England–South Africa, and again a Vickers Vimy was used for the first attempt. Two South Africans, Pierre van Ryneveld and Quintin Brand, left Brooklands on March 11, 1920, only to crash on the Egyptian border. They continued in another Vimy, crashed again, and finally completed the journey in a de Havilland D.H.9, arriving in Cape Town on 20 March.

Empire pioneers

The possibility of regular services to the countries of the then British Empire grew stronger when Sir Alan Cobham began his series of trailblazing flights. At first he used a de Havilland D.H.50 powered by a 335 hp Armstrong-Siddeley Jaguar

Hawker took off from Newfoundland on May 18, 1919, and almost immediately ran into terrible weather. The engine cooling system failed and finally, after 2,240 km (1,400 miles), Hawker and his navigator made a forced landing and were picked up by a Danish ship.

A month later, two more Englishmen accepted the challenge. The pilot was Captain John Alcock, his navigator Lieutenant Arthur Whitten Brown, and their mount yet another Vickers Vimy. After battling through thick fog, they sighted the Irish coast ahead and Alcock decided to land. He chose what seemed a level piece of ground, but the aeroplane ended its historic flight with its nose buried deep in an Irish bog and its tail raised forlornly to the sky. Fortunately both men were unhurt, having flown 3,023 km (1,890 miles) in 15 hours 57 minutes and proved that aeroplane services across the Atlantic were more than possible — they were inevitable.

The first non-stop crossing of the South Atlantic was made in a Breguet XIX piloted by two French aviators, Dieudonné Costes and Lieutenant le Brix. For 1927 their machine was interesting — a single-engined biplane of all-metal construction except for the fabric covering its wings and tail. A flight lasting 20 hours 50 minutes took the two Frenchmen from St Louis to Port Natal, Brazil, a distance of 3,220 km (2,000 miles).

That year also saw what remains to this day the most celebrated long-distance solo flight in the history of aviation. On May 20, 1927, a 24-year-old American named Charles Lindbergh took off from New York and headed across the Atlantic towards Paris. His aeroplane, a Ryan NYP powered by a single 237 hp Wright J-5C Whirlwind radial, was exceptionally small for such a crossing. It had a wing span of only 14 m (46 ft) and a maximum speed of 200 km/h (124 mph). After 28 interminable hours Lindbergh sighted the coast of Ireland, and 5½ hours later his aeroplane, the *Spirit of St Louis*, touched down at Le Bourget near Paris after a flight covering 5,776 km (3,610 miles).

In August 1931 another great pilot, Jim Mollison, crossed the Atlantic from Ireland to Nova Scotia in a D.H.80A Puss Moth. In February of the following year he flew from Lympne, Southern England, to Rio de Janeiro in 3½ days, becoming the first aviator to cross the North and South Atlantic solo. His aeroplane belonged to the de Havilland Moth family, aircraft which revolutionized private flying. The first D.H. Moth flew early in 1925, powered by a 60 hp ADC Cirrus 1 four-cylinder engine driving a two-bladed propeller 1.93 m (6 ft 4 in) in diameter. This classic design attracted attention almost as soon as it appeared: the British Air Ministry subsidised a number of flying clubs, equipping them with

Moths. A whole generation of men and women flew these de Havilland biplanes for pleasure, and the fighter pilots who were later to prevail over Southern England and the Channel received their initial training on them.

Flying ladies

Surprisingly, in view of the role usually assigned to women at that time, the first female pilot was granted a pilot's licence in 1909, the year that the Frenchman Blériot flew the English Channel. She too was French — her name was Mme la Baronne de Laroche — and her aeroplane was a Voisin powered by an ENV Type F 60 hp engine driving a two-bladed pusher propeller. The first British woman qualified two years later — Mrs Hilda Hewlett, holder of licence No 122, learned on a Farman powered by a 50 hp Gnome rotary engine and capable of a maximum speed of 60 km/h (37 mph).

World War I meant the end of private flying, but women began to hit the headlines as soon as hostilities ended. Among them were Mrs Keith Miller, the first woman to fly to Australia; Lady Heath and Lady Bailey, both of whom flew independently from England to Cape Town; and the inimitable Amy Johnson, a great recordbreaker.

Above The de Havilland Puss Moth of 1929, a three-seater, high-wing cabin monoplane, one of the company's series of light training aircraft.

Right The Supermarine S-6, a cantilever monoplane which won the Schneider Trophy outright for Great Britain in 1929.

All of them used small, popular types such as the Avro Avian and de Havilland Moth.

America's most famous woman pilot was Amelia Earhart, who in May 1932 became the first woman to fly solo across the Atlantic. She flew a Lockheed Vega from Newfoundland to Northern Ireland, adding to the already formidable reputation enjoyed by this fine machine. The Vega was also used during the 1930s by other aviation eminences, among them Wiley Post, Harold Gatty, James Mattern and polar explorer Sir Hubert Wilkins. Powered by a 450 hp Pratt & Whitney Wasp C engine, the Vega cruised at 274 km/h (170 mph) over a range of 885 km (550 miles).

The quest for speed

World War I apart, the greatest inducements towards the development of faster and faster aircraft during aviation's first three decades were the great international speed trophies. In 1913 the race for the Gordon Bennett Aviation Trophy was won by a Deperdussin monoplane. The experience gained in pursuit of this prize enabled the company to build the Spad series, the fastest fighters of World War I.

The first race for the Schneider Trophy for high-speed seaplanes, held in 1913, was won by a Deperdussin at a speed of 73.2 km/h (45.75 mph). After the war the Schneider competition attracted government-sponsored entries from all over Europe. Nine races took place from 1920 to 1931, until the trophy was won outright by Britain after three consecutive victories. The winning aeroplane that year was a Supermarine S-6B, developed from the Supermarine S-5 designed by R. J. Mitchell for the 1927 race. From the S-6B was developed the Spitfire, one of the most successful aeroplanes of World War II.

The greatest air race of all time was the contest for the MacRobertson Trophy, flown between England and Australia in 1934. Out of an original entry of 70, only 20 aircraft came to the starting line. Three of the British entries were specially built de Havilland Comets fitted with twin 230 hp Gipsy engines. One of these, piloted by C. W. A. Scott and T. Campbell Black, arrived first, having covered the 18,080 km (11,300 miles) course in just under three days at an average speed of 256 km/h (160 mph). Two Americans, Turner and Pangborn, came in second in a Boeing, and Cathcart-Jones and Waller were third in another Comet. First in the handicap race were two Dutchmen, Parmentier and Moll in a KLM Douglas DC-2.

Scheduled services

The DC-2 exemplified a generation of airliners which was to set design fashions for the next two decades and beyond. The first, the Ford Tri-motor of 1926, represented a great improvement over the biplanes of the time, combining a high-set cantilever wing with a corrugated-metal load-bearing skin and three-engined reliability. These techniques made possible a clean, strong structure capable of flying faster, further and more safely than the biplanes, held back as they were by the 'built-in headwind' generated by myriads of struts and bracing wires.

A 'Tin Goose', as the Tri-motor came to be known, was used for the first pioneering flight over the South Pole on November 28, 1929, and isolated examples continued in commercial service well into the 1970s.

Technically similar to the Tri-motor but rather more refined was Germany's Junkers Ju52, which first flew in 1931. Incorporating a low-set cranked wing fitted with extensive trailing-edge flaps, the Ju52 first entered service with some of Europe's international airlines. But it was as the military 'Tante Ju' ('Auntie Ju') that this Junkers design earned its international reputation. Variants served with the Luftwaffe throughout World War II, dropping paratroops in the mass airborne assault on Crete and supplying the beleaguered German armies on the Eastern Front. The type was also licence-built in Spain, and a handful are still on charge with the Spanish Air Force.

Though the Boeing 247 never equalled the enormous commercial success of its DC-3 near-contemporary, this low-wing twin-engined monoplane featured a number of innovations which were to revolutionize airliner design. The 247's undercarriage could be retracted to reduce drag during the cruise. Blade pitch could be varied to maximise propeller efficiency for various phases of flight, and small auxiliary surfaces (tabs) on the elevators, ailerons and rudder made it possible to trim the aircraft in flight so that it could be controlled for long periods by an autopilot. And to counter dangerous ice build-ups, the wing leading edges and the tail were fitted with de-icing equipment.

But ironically it was the Boeing 247's technical success which put paid to its chances in the market place. The ten-passenger 247 entered service with United Airlines in March 1933, immediately cutting trans-USA journey time to under 20 hours for the first time. Transcontinental & Western Air, United's main rival, realized that equipment at least as good as the 247 would have to be bought if it was to stay in business. A deal with Boeing was out of the question, such was the closeness of the Seattle manufacturer's relationship with United. So it was that Transcontinental approached Douglas with a specification which led to the DC-1,

progenitor of the MacRobertson-winning DC-2 and of the immortal DC-3.

Embodying all the advanced technology of the Boeing 247, plus increased passenger capacity, the DC-3 first flew in 1935. By December 1941 no fewer than eight in ten of all US domestic scheduled airlines operated DC-3s, and the type was in massive series production for the US forces and the RAF. The former knew the DC-3 mainly as the C-47 or 'Gooney Bird', while the British dubbed it the Dakota. Battle honours included the 'Hump' airlift over the Himalayas between India and China, and the series of airborne attacks in North-western Europe during 1944 and 1945. Production exceeded 10,000, of which almost a thousand remain in military and commercial service worldwide.

At the end of World War I Britain appeared to have a great aviation advantage over other nations. She had the men, the machines and something like 700 bases and airfields. With very little effort, it seemed, she could achieve world leadership in commercial aviation.

Yet, curiously, the first European nation to begin civil airline operations was the supposedly crushed and beaten Germany. On February 5, 1919, the world's first daily passenger air service was begun,

Far left The twin-tail Lockheed Electra of 1934, a twin-engined, ten passenger monoplane airliner. This was one of the first commercial aircraft to be fitted with de-icing equipment.

Above 'Hengist', one of the Imperial Airways' fleet of Handley Page HP.42 Hannibals, used on the London-Paris route during the 1930's. They carried up to 38 people in a luxurious interior.

Left A painting by Kenneth McDonough depicting a Handley Page W.8b Royal Mail airliner of Imperial Airways taxiing across Plough Lane next to Croydon Airport in the early 1930s.

using five-seater AEG biplanes and DFW two-seaters. Other countries soon followed suit, and passenger, mail and freight-carrying companies began to form around the world.

On August 25, 1919, E. H. Lawford made the world's first scheduled international flight from Hounslow to Le Bourget. His aeroplane was a D.H.4A, a converted light bomber powered by a single 350 hp Rolls-Royce Eagle VIII and capable of covering 402 km (250 miles) without refuelling. Lawford carried one passenger, and a consignment of leather, Devonshire cream, mail and several brace of grouse. The operator was Aircraft Transport & Travel Ltd, originally founded in 1916. Eight days later, Handley Page Transport Ltd began a cross-Channel scheduled service to Paris, followed on September 23, 1919, by a route to Brussels. The world's first scheduled airlines operated converted twin-engined Handley Page 0/400 bombers.

Companies with names familiar even now were formed by amalgamating small, struggling companies. Imperial Airways is a good example of this trend, emerging in March 1924 from the coalescence of Handley Page Transport, Instone Air Line Ltd, Daimler Airway and British Marine Air Navigation. Almost immediately, Imperial made a survey flight to India, and by 1929 Britain's first long-range route, London to Karachi, had been established. By 1932 it had been extended southward to Africa, and then eastward in 1934 to Australia in conjunction with Qantas, the Australian airline. In 1933 the decision to allow

Imperial Airways to carry Empire mail helped it achieve leading international airline status.

Transatlantic flights started in August 1939 and, although the Second World War ended that activity, within the next few months Imperial was reorganized, merging with British Airways to form the State-owned British Overseas Airways Corporation (BOAC). During its fifteen years of existence Imperial Airways flew a variety of aircraft including the famous but outdated Handley Page HP.42. These great four-engined biplanes carried 39 passengers, cruising at 152 km/h (93 mph) over a range of 480 km (300 miles). Later Imperial took delivery of its first Armstrong Whitworth AW.15 Atlantas. With a cruising speed of 208 km/h (130 mph), this type presented passengers with the first major reduction in journey time since 1919.

The flying-boat years

It was perhaps this desire for increased speed that eventually ended the ten-year reign of the flying boat. Seaplanes were first used for civil aviation because they seemed to offer increased safety when flying long distances over the sea. In time, floats gave way to fuselages designed to hydrodynamic principles and capable of floating and moving at high speed over the water. In 1924 Francesco de Pinedo flew from Italy to Australia and Japan and back in a Savoia-Marchetti S.16, and between December 17, 1930, and January 14, 1931, Balbo led 12 S.55s on the first formation flight across the Atlantic. He repeated the feat two years later with 24 similar craft.

Right A CP Air Douglas DC-3. This aircraft was first produced in 1935 for both civil and military use, and there are still many in service today with commercial airlines throughout the world.

Above right The Boeing 247, introduced in 1933. This aircraft, a well-streamlined low-wing monoplane with twin engines, was the forerunner of the modern airliner.

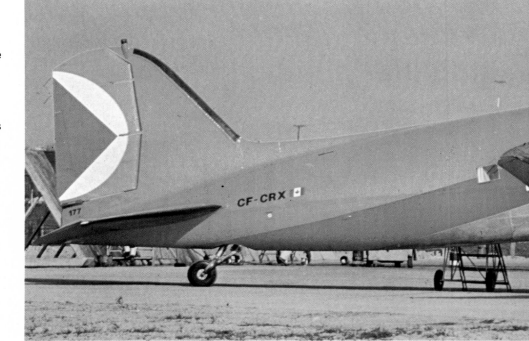

Above A Sikorsky S.42 flying boat. It was an aircraft of this type which carried out the first survey flight from America to New Zealand, and they were used mainly on the Pacific routes.

Right The first regular passenger service across the North Atlantic was inaugurated on 8 July 1939, using this type of flying boat, the 42-ton Boeing Model 314. The service was, however, dropped during World War II.

These achievements did much to foster public confidence in the flying boat, and by the late 1920s and early 1930s it seemed as if they would dominate long-distance travel. In Britain, the Short Calcutta entered service in 1928, carrying mail within the British Empire. In 1931 Imperial Airways introduced the Short Kent, regarded as the most comfortable airliner of its day, followed in 1938 by the Short C-class Empire flying boats. They were powered by Perseus XII engines, had a speed of 322 km/h (200 mph) and carried 24 passengers.

An unusual aircraft of the time was the Short-Mayo Composite, a large flying boat (*Maia*) which carried 'pick-a-back' a small floated mailplane known as *Mercury*. It was planned that *Maia* would extend the fully laden *Mercury's* range by carrying it to cruising height before releasing it to continue the journey unaided. In the event, the Composite never entered regular service.

Germany also built some fine flying boats during the inter-war years, the most spectacular of which was the 12-engined Dornier DoX, a veritable giant with a wingspan of 48 m (157 ft 6 in) and accommodation for nearly 170 passengers. Dornier Wal flying boats were used to maintain the Deutsche Lufthansa service across the South Atlantic. The Wals were supported by floating aerodromes — two converted liners and the specially designed *Ostmark* — stationed in mid-ocean.

America also was a great proponent of the flying boat. In 1927 Consolidated Commodores were being used on routes between Key West, Florida, and Havana, Cuba, a distance of 177 km (110 miles). The Sikorsky S.42 of 1934, built to a Pan Am specification, was the first US airliner capable of making long sea crossings. It had a range of 4,828 km (3,000 miles) at a speed of 292 km/h (182 mph) and carried 32 passengers. Perhaps the most famous of all American flying boats was the Martin M.130 *China Clipper*, which carried 46 passengers to inaugurate the San Francisco-Honolulu-Manila route.

The great international airlines

Nevertheless, despite these later successes, the early US airlines had had problems. Would-be passengers studied the alternative form of transport — rail — and usually decided to travel that way. The early aeroplanes were snail-like by modern standards, 128 km/h (80 mph) being a fair average, and none could equal the luxury offered by American Pullman trains. Consequently, most of the aviation enterprises of the time concentrated on airmail services.

Matters improved with the appearance of new aircraft, and then in 1927 Pan American Airways came into being. Progress thereafter was exceedingly rapid. From operating a single 176 km (110 miles) route in its first year, Pan Am began to grow into a great airline. Steps on the way were services to the Caribbean and South America, an Atlantic route projected in 1937, and flights to Alaska the following year. By 1939 the company had a network of routes more extensive than that of any leading European airline, many of which had been in operation since the early 1920s.

In Europe, airlines were proliferating. Four of the most important were KLM, founded in 1919, Sabena in 1923, Lufthansa in 1926 and Air France in 1933. They were equipped mainly with Junkers, Savoia-Marchetti, Douglas, Fokker and Lockheed aircraft. By the middle 1930s, many of the 'civilian' aircraft were being built with an eye to immediate conversion to military configuration should the

need arise. And by September 1939 that need had arisen, with the outbreak of World War II.

Destruction from the air

The temporary aversion to everything military which followed World War I had the effect of reversing the evolutionary sequence established during the early years of heavier-than-air flight. From 1903 to 1918 the air arms of Europe and America had at least as great an influence on the progress of aviation as did civilian interests. Indeed, for the four years of the war the energies of the world's aircraft industries were expended almost exclusively on the production of ever more effective warplanes. The Armistice changed all that: far from being the pace-setter, military flying lagged behind civil aviation as governments cut spending on their air forces to the minimum.

The development of military aircraft between the wars fell into three phases: a period when the air forces had to soldier on with war-surplus equipment was followed by the zenith of the biplane's career, which ended with the advent of the first effective fighting monoplanes. In the early 1920s the air forces of the European colonial powers carried out police actions in the Sudan, Iraq, India's North-west Frontier and Morocco using World War I-vintage Bristol Fighters, D.H.4s,

D.H.9s and Breguet 14s. On the other side of the Atlantic, the US Marines were using D.H.4s against Nicaraguan rebels as late as 1927.

Then, when at last it was decided to make more money available for the production of new fighters and bombers, there began a cautious process of development which saw the biplane fighter refined to the limits of its potential. Perhaps the best example of this second phase was the beautiful Fairey Fantôme. Destined never to enter squadron service, this Belgian-designed fighter was one of the cleanest biplanes ever built. Powered by an 850 hp Hispano engine, the prototype Fantôme first flew from Fairey's Gosselies airfield in 1935, ultimately proving capable of about 354 km/h (220 mph) at sea level, 435 km/h (270 mph) at height, and 700 km (435 miles) range at 350 km/h (217 mph).

In Britain fighting craft such as the Gloster Gamecock and Bristol Bulldog made their debut, as did a range of bombers including the Vickers Wellesley, the Handley Page W.10, and the Boulton Paul Overstrand.

Elsewhere, other countries were also persisting with the biplane formula when it was becoming increasingly obvious that the monoplane was the right way to go, as the airliner manufacturers of the US and Germany had already discovered. The RAF fighter units of the time were equipped with such satisfactory but relatively unadventurous types as the Hawker Fury. Comparable aircraft in service with the other advanced air forces in the world included Japan's Kawasaki Type 99 light bomber; the German Heinkel He51, which was to serve with the Nationalists during the Spanish Civil War, and its Italian comrade-in-arms, the Fiat CR 32.

But though in the main the military designers were taking fewer chances than the best of their commercial counterparts, there were a few notable exceptions. It was the bomber — rather than the traditionally faster and more technically demanding fighter — which spearheaded the switch to the monoplane layout. Pioneering designs included the Russian Tupolev TB-1, which took to the air in 1927 to become the world's first multi-engined monoplane bomber. Powered by a pair of licence-built German engines and owing much to the stressed-skin techniques developed by Junkers for the Ju52, the all-metal TB-1 could carry a bomb load of 1,000 kg (2,200 lb) at 208 km/h (130 mph).

In 1932 came Boeing's B-9, the first twin-

engined monoplane bomber to be fitted with a retractable undercarriage. It could cruise at 300 km/h (188 mph) and represented a great advance over the Vickers Virginia biplanes then in service with the RAF. Slower than the B-9 but with twice the bomb load over twice the range, the Tupolev TB-3 was the world's first four-engined bomber.

By 1936, largely as a result of the widely held belief that formations of fast, heavily armed bombers would always defeat defensive fighter opposi-tion, funds were being diverted into bomber development. This doctrine gave rise to a genera-tion of bombers capable of showing a clean pair of heels to most of the fighters then extant. Two such were the 415 km/h (260 mph) Tupolev SB-2 and the 427 km/h (267 mph) S.79 from Italy's Savoia-Marchetti.

The supremacy of the bomber was short-lived, however. First of a new breed of fast, manoeuvrable fighter was the Soviet Polikarpov I-16 Type 1.

Left One of the world's best-known transport aircraft, the Junkers Ju52/3m. This is another example of an all-metal monoplane with a corrugated metal skin to carry some of the load.

Below The Ford Tri-motor. The design was based on the Fokker FVII/3m three-engined high-wing monoplane, except that it was all-metal, including its corrugated skin, which earned it the name 'Tin Goose'.

Above A contemporary colour photograph of the Boeing YI B-17, introduced in 1937. This was a strategic bomber used by the USAAC.

Right One of the most popular flying trainers in the U.S. was the Stearman Kaydet (1934). It was eventually used in large numbers by the Air Force.

Deserving credit as the first fighter to combine a cantilevered wing with a retractable undercarriage, the I-16 was nevertheless an undistinguished example of a formidable species. Capable of a maximum speed of only 358 km/h (224 mph), the I-16 was badly underpowered, a deficiency finally corrected by the substitution of a 775 hp licence-built American engine for the original Soviet powerplant. Top speed went up to 450 km/h (280 mph), enabling the I-16 to give a good account of itself against Nationalist He51s at the beginning of the Spanish Civil War.

The year 1936 proved a time of great activity in Britain. The Armstrong Whitworth Whitley, Vickers Wellington and Handley Page Hampden monoplane bombers made their first flights, as did that result of the Schneider Trophy races, the Supermarine Spitfire.

Fighting in Abyssinia (1935–1936) and in Spain (1936–1939) gave Italian and then German aeroplanes actual combat experience before World War II broke out in September 1939. Soon, fighter battles were taking place in the skies over Britain and Western Europe, and hundreds and then thousands of bombers were to drone through the night skies to bring death and destruction to many great cities.

Chapter 4
WORLD WAR II

J UST as World War II outdid even the First in destructive scale and extent, so too did it force the evolution of aircraft along at an unprecedented pace. In September 1939 the front-line units arrayed against one another in Western Europe were equipped mainly with piston-engined monoplane fighters and twin-motor medium-range bombers. Six years later, after a ferocious development race in which the defeated Axis powers had played a brilliant if ultimately futile part, swept-wing jet and rocket fighters were rattling the bars of the sound barrier, four-engined pressurized bombers spanned oceans, and a wealth of technology lay waiting to be exploited.

One type had come to the end of the road, however, during the war. The piston-engined aircraft was refined and updated to its most sophisticated limits until the phenomenon of compressibility put paid to the propeller and straight wing as means of reaching the highest speeds.

Fighters

Nevertheless, the piston-engined, single-seat monoplane fighter enjoyed a successful war, dominating the daylight air battles between 1939 and 1945. None of the species had flown long before 1935, and 1939 saw their first large-scale operations. By 1945, however, the breed had passed its peak and was on the way to extinction.

The first of the single-engined classics took off for the first time from Augsburg in Southern Germany in September 1935. The first Messerschmitt Bf109 was powered by a Rolls-Royce Kestrel engine as no suitable German powerplant was available. Early production versions fought in the Spanish Civil War with the Condor Legion, the unit which provided the resurgent Luftwaffe with its first fighting experience. These Bf109Bs were powered by Junkers Jumo 210 engines and were mostly relegated to second-line and training units by the time war broke out.

The German Messerschmitt Bf109, a fighter with an incomparable reputation. It first proved its worth during the Spanish Civil War.

The first major production Bf109 was the Bf109E, with the Daimler-Benz DB601 engine giving 1,100 hp. Some E-series aircraft carried a 20 mm MG FF cannon (a version of the Swiss Oerlikon) mounted between the cylinder banks of the inverted V-12 engine and firing through the hub, but standard armament was two MG FFs in the outer wings and two 7.9 mm MG 17s above the engine. Top speed was 570 km/h (354 mph) attained at 12,300 ft altitude. Notable features of the Bf109 included its relatively small wing with automatic leading-edge slots to improve low-speed handling. The fact that the DB601 used direct fuel injection rather than carburettors gave the Bf109 an advantage over its opponents — the 109 could dive faster than an adversary because the opponent's engine would be starved of fuel under negative gravitational forces as he pushed the nose down.

The Bf109E established a high reputation in the first months of the war; it was not until the Battle of Britain that it met the Spitfire, the only aircraft among its contemporaries which could face it on equal terms. Its only basic drawback was a very small landing-gear track, which made it tricky to handle on the ground.

The peak of Bf109 development, many pilots felt, was reached with the Bf109F in early 1941. The wing-mounted MG FF cannon were removed and an uprated DB601 giving 1,300 hp was fitted. The new version could touch nearly 630 km/h (390 mph) at altitude, but, more important, could also match the Spitfire's turning circle because of extended wingtips and modified ailerons.

By the end of 1942, however, the failure of the German industry to produce a replacement for the Bf109 was making itself felt. The Bf109G, with heavier armament than the F-series and the bigger 1,475 hp DB605 engine, weighed up to 3,500 kg (7,500 lb) compared with 2,500 kg (5,500 lb) for the Bf109E. Inevitably, flying characteristics suffered, although top speed went up to more than 725 km/h (450 mph) in later versions. Production of the

Bf109 lasted until the war's end (and continued in Spain and Czechoslovakia) and more than 30,000 were built.

The first Hawker Hurricane flew in November 1935, two months later than the Bf109. In some respects its design was less advanced than that of the German fighter or the Supermarine Spitfire: it had evolved from a design based on the Fury biplane fighter and retained the traditional fabric covering for wings and fuselage. Although such features limited the Hurricane's performance, they allowed production to build up swiftly, and the RAF had far more Hurricanes than Spitfires when France fell in June 1940.

The Hurricane I was powered by a 1,030 hp Rolls-Royce Merlin III, the engine that powered so many of the Allies' most important aircraft. It gave the Hurricane a top speed of 520 km/h (324 mph) at

Right The Hawker Hurricane, one of the RAF's first eight-gun monoplane fighters. These quickly superseded the earlier monoplane types.

Below right A squadron of Messerschmitt Bf109s.

Below The Gloster Gladiator, the last biplane fighter of the RAF. It was highly manoeuvrable and capable of a top speed of 407 km/h (253 mph).

16,250 ft. In contrast to the cannon and two machine-guns of the Bf109, the Hurricane's armament comprised eight 0.303 in Colt-Browning machine-guns installed in the wings.

Hurricanes served in many theatres of war, often in roles very different from their design mission. They were catapulted off merchant ships to shoot down marauding Fw200 Kurier patrol aircraft. One was tested with a jettisonable, fuel-carrying auxiliary wing to increase range. Armament of later Hurricanes was increased to four 20 mm Oerlikon cannon, and the Hurricane IID tank-buster carried two 40 mm cannon under the wings. The last Hurricane was delivered in September 1944 and over 14,000 were built.

The Hurricane's team-mate, the Supermarine Spitfire, was designed to the same eight-gun, Merlin-powered formula, but stayed in production and under active development throughout the war, the only Allied fighter to do so. It was more advanced than the Hurricane, being of all-metal, stressed-skin construction throughout.

The Spitfire flew in March 1936 and the Royal Air Force started to receive quantities of the initial Spitfire IA in May 1938. The IA attained nearly 590 km/h (365 mph) at altitude on the power of a 1,030 hp Merlin II or III. Armament was the same eight Colt-Brownings as were fitted to the Hurricane.

The Spitfire I was faster than the Messerschmitt Bf109 in level flight, although the German fighter could climb and dive faster. The Spitfire had a clear superiority in turning performance at all altitudes.

Development of new Spitfire versions could be given higher priority with the ending of the Battle of Britain, and in March 1941 the more powerful Spitfire VB began to reach the squadrons. Power-plant was the Merlin 45, fitted with a more effective supercharger and giving 1,470 hp. The VB was particularly suited to low-level operations, and many aircraft of this type were built with clipped, square-cut wingtips to make them faster at low altitude.

The Spitfire IX was built in larger numbers than any other variant of the type. Paradoxically, it was

Far left below The Junkers Ju87 (Stuka) which Germany used as a close-support aircraft during the *Blitzkrieg* in 1939/40. However, they were no match for the British Hurricanes and Spitfires.

Left The Heinkel He111 remained in service throughout the war in a variety of activities, including torpedo-bombing, pathfinding, glider-tugging, launching V-1 missiles and transporting cargo.

Below The Supermarine Spitfire. This aircraft is remembered chiefly for its performance in the Battle of Britain, where its high speed and manoeuvrability were of the greatest importance.

developed as a stop-gap when the arrival of the Focke-Wulf Fw190 led to a demand for a quickly available, faster Spitfire. The Merlin was hotted-up again; with the Merlin 60 rated at 1,710 hp the Spitfire IX attained 650 km/h (404 mph) making it one of the fastest fighter aircraft of the time. Standard armament on the Mark IX was two 20 mm Hispano cannon and four Colt-Brownings. 5,600 of a total of 22,000 Spitfires were Mark IXs.

Development of the Spitfire did not stop with the Mark IX. The next step was a switch to the Merlin's bigger stablemate, the Rolls-Royce Griffon, which was fitted to the Marks XII and XIV. Late-production Spitfire XIVs introduced a cut-down rear fuselage and a bubble canopy to give the pilot a better view. Just as the war ended in Europe the first RAF squadron was working up with the Spitfire 21. This version could touch 731 km/h (454 mph) on the power of a 2,050 hp Griffon 61 — that is to say, the Mark 21 was almost exactly twice as powerful as the original Spitfire I. The Spitfire 21 introduced a strengthened wing and, for the first time, carried an armament of four 20 mm Hispano cannon.

Airborne destroyers

By no means all military theorists before the war believed that the single-seat, single-engined fighter would decide the air battle. A lot of effort was put into developing 'destroyers' — heavily armed, twin-engined fighters which, it was thought, could outgun the single-seaters, carry out long offensive patrols and escort bombers.

Some members of the German air staff placed great faith in the Messerschmitt Me110, first flown in May 1936. The production Me110C entered service in January 1939, powered by DB601s. It carried a crew of three, and was armed with two 20 mm MG FF cannon and two 7.9 mm MG17 machine-guns fixed to fire forward, and one MG 17 on a flexible mounting at the rear of the long, greenhouse-like canopy. Top speed at 20,000 ft was 541 km/h (336 mph) and range was 1,100 km (680 miles).

But when the 'destroyers' went into action in the Battle of Britain it was found that they could neither outrun nor outmanoeuvre the single-seat fighters and that the defensive machine-gun was pitifully inadequate. Following heavy losses, the Me110 was withdrawn from daylight operations where single-seat fighters were to be found. Later in the war the Me110 redeemed its reputation on night-fighter duties, for which a twin-engined, two-seat aircraft was needed to carry and make use of cumbersome intercept radar. In fact Me110 production, halted after the Battle of Britain, had to be restarted in 1942 with the Me110G night-fighter, powered by 1,475 hp DB605s and sprouting a complex array of radar aerials on the nose and wings.

Britain never experimented with the day-fighting 'destroyer', but used the twin-engined Bristol Beaufighter as a night fighter and anti-shipping aircraft. It went into service in September 1940, just as the night raids on London got under way. It was a powerful machine, with two 1,590 hp Bristol Hercules radial engines, and carried a heavy armament of four 20 mm Hispano cannon and six 0.303 in Colt-Browning guns. Some Beaufighters were fitted with Merlins because of a shortage of Hercules.

From 1942 the Mosquito started to replace the Beaufighter in the night-fighter role and the Beaufighter was seen as more of a long-range day fighter and anti-shipping aircraft, armed with bombs, torpedoes and rockets. Nearly 6,000 Beaufighters were built, and production was starting in Australia as the war ended.

The American 'destroyer' was the Lockheed P-38 Lightning, one of the most technically advanced aircraft of the war. The nacelles of the two Allison V-1710 engines extended rearwards to form slim booms which carried the tail unit and

accommodated exhaust-driven turbosuperchargers. The Lightning had a tricycle undercarriage and the wing flaps could be used to tighten the turning radius. The Lightning's high speed and altitude — 676 km/h (420 mph) at 25,000 ft — meant that the type did not have to fight unless conditions were favourable, and it established an excellent record as an escort fighter.

France and Italy were well to the fore in aviation technology in the 1930s, but neither managed to develop advanced fighters before the outbreak of war. France had flown the single-engined Morane-Saulnier MS.406 in August 1935 and it was the most numerous fighter available to the French in September 1939. Although it was built at the same time as the Bf109 and the British fighters, it was less powerful and slower, with a maximum speed of only 486 km/h (302 mph). It was powered by an 860 hp Hispano-Suiza 12Y engine and carried an armament of one 20 mm cannon and two machine-guns.

Typical of early Italian fighters was the Fiat G.50. Although it had made its first flight later than the Spitfire, in February 1937, the G.50 was an earlier type of aeroplane, with an open cockpit and low-powered radial engine. Armament was two 0.5 in Breda-SAFAT machine-guns.

Above The Grumman F4F-3 Wildcat, the company's first mid-wing monoplane fighter, usually flown from aircraft carriers.

Right The Lockheed P-38 Lightning, first introduced in 1941 and used for long-range escort duties for bombers over Germany and the Pacific.

Like the French and Italian air forces the US Navy was under-equipped when it was precipitated into war by the attack on Pearl Harbour. The USA had neglected the single-engined fighter, and the USN's Grumman F4F Wildcat and Brewster F2A Buffalo were slower and less well-armed than the latest European fighters. Their air-cooled radial engines created more drag than the sleekly cowled liquid-cooled inline types, and neither fighter could exceed 515 km/h (320 mph). The Wildcat achieved some successes with the British Fleet Air Arm as the Martlet, however, and in the Pacific four Wildcats took part in the doomed defence of Wake Island. Both the Wildcat and the Buffalo (which saw service in Finland) carried a standard armament of four 0.5 in machine-guns — the classic 'fifty-calibre' which armed nearly every US aircraft.

The US Army Air Force had made an attempt to introduce a single-engined fighter comparable to the Bf109 and Spitfire by adapting the radial-engined Curtiss Hawk to take the V-12, liquid-cooled Allison V-1710. The result was the Curtiss P-40 series, of which some 13,800 were built between 1939 and 1944. The P-40 was regarded as a useful low-altitude fighter, and the RAF used the early Tomahawk for close support. Above 15,000 ft the power of the mechanically supercharged V-1710 (as opposed to the turbosupercharged version of the same engine fitted to the P-38) dropped sharply, and this limited the P-40's usefulness.

The early P-40B (Tomahawk to the RAF) attained 563 km/h (352 mph) at 15,000 ft on the 1,150 hp available from its engine. Armament comprised two 0.5 in and two 0.303 in machine-guns. Later P-40s (which the RAF called Kittyhawks and the USAAF called Warhawks) had more powerful engines — Merlins in the P-40F — and up to six 0.5 in guns.

At the outbreak of war in the Pacific the Wildcats, Buffaloes and early P-40s of the US services were outclassed by the Japanese Navy and Air Force fighters. Foremost among these was the Japanese Navy Air Force's Mitsubishi A6M Type 0 Zero fighter — usually known simply as the Zero-Sen. Although like its US opponents it had a fairly small radial engine — a 925 hp Mitsubishi Sakae — it was fast, with a top speed of 545 km/h (338 mph). Its remarkable 2,400 km (1,500 miles) range was useful in the Pacific, and it carried two

20 mm Type 99 cannon and two machine-guns. Its main asset was superb manoeuvrability, and even the Spitfire could not beat it in a close-quarters dogfight. Later in the war its lack of armour and self-sealing tanks started to tell against it, but at the time of Pearl Harbour it was unbeatable. Its land-based counterpart in the Imperial Japanese Air Force was the Nakajima Ki.43 Hayabusa, less heavily armed but with similar manoeuvrability, aided by combat flaps.

Not only in the Pacific was the fighter battle going against the Allies. In July 1942 the Focke-Wulf Fw190A entered service, and it was soon realised that the new fighter had an edge over all its contemporaries. Designed as the smallest aircraft which could use the big 1,600 hp BMW 801 radial, the Fw190 could fly at 663 km/h (412 mph) with emergency boost. It carried two 20 mm, drum-fed MG FF cannon in the outer wings, two belt-fed MG 151s of similar calibre in the wing roots and two machine-guns in the fuselage. The basic radial-engined Fw190 fighter-bomber carried bombs as heavy as 1,800 kg (3,970 lb). As a 'bomber destroyer' it carried up to six 20 mm cannon in and under its wings. The Fw190G, with a BMW 801 giving 1,870 hp, could touch 575 km/h (356 mph) at sea level, compared with 507 km/h (312 mph) for the Fw190A.

Even faster was the Fw190D-9, which entered

L.488335

Above The Republic P-47N Thunderbolt, a long-range American fighter which came into service in 1944 and was used in the Pacific.

Left The Me163B Komet, a single-seat rocket-propelled interceptor fighter powered by the dangerous Walter bi-fuel liquid rocket unit.

Above right Germany's first operational turbojet aircraft, the Messerschmitt Me262, developed as a fighter-bomber and used from October 1944 onwards.

service in 1944 powered by a Junkers Jumo 213 rated at 2,240 hp with water/methanol boost. The Dora-9 could fly at 685 km/h (425 mph).

High-speed fighters

Fortunately for the Allies, their designers had not neglected the design of comparable 'second-generation' aircraft. One of the first to appear was the Hawker Tornado, which flew in October 1939, powered by a 1,760 hp Rolls-Royce Vulture. The

Possibly the best all-round fighter of the war was an early example of Anglo-American collaboration. The North American NA-73 was designed and flown in 1940 at the request of a British purchasing delegation. It had a single Allison V-1710 and featured a laminar-flow aerofoil which gave the new fighter exceptionally high performance and long range. Designated P-51A (Mustang 1 to the RAF), the new fighter entered service in April 1942. With a 1,200 hp Allison engine it could achieve 630 km/h (390 mph) at altitude, and had a range of more than 3,200 km (2,000 miles).

Like the P-40, the early Mustang was limited in altitude performance by the Allison engine, and it only realised its full potential when fitted with a Packard-built Rolls-Royce Merlin. The P-51B which resulted had a top speed of 710 km/h (440 mph) at 30,000 ft on the power of a 1,695 hp Merlin, and deliveries of P-51Bs to the USAAF started at the end of 1943. Late in 1944 the 3,750 P-51Bs were followed by the first P-51Ds with bubble hood and cut-down rear fuselage.

The USAAF's other main single-engined fighter was the massive Republic P-47 Thunderbolt, more than three times as heavy as the original Spitfire I. Like the Mustang, it incorporated the lessons of 1940, but it was built around a 2,000 hp-plus Pratt & Whitney R-2800 radial engine, with air and gas ducting from and to an exhaust-driven turbosupercharger passing beneath the pilot's seat and the wing. First flown in May 1941, the P-47 entered service on escort and fighter-sweep missions in Europe in March 1943.

The main production version of the Thunderbolt was the P-47D, built with and without the all-round-vision bubble hood. The firepower was remarkable — the armament was eight 0.5 in machine-guns — and because of its weight the

Vulture was however cancelled in mid-1941, and Hawker shifted its efforts to the Typhoon, which used the 2,100 hp Napier Sabre and flew in February 1940. It was brought into service in September 1941, but was plagued with structural problems and troubles with the complex 24-cylinder, 'horizontal-H' Sabre. The Sabre engine suffered from poor performance at high altitude, so the Typhoon was used mainly for close support. Armed with up to eight 27 kg (60 lb) rockets, it proved a devastating anti-tank weapon. The Typhoon was succeeded by the Tempest, with a thinner, 'laminar-flow' wing to avoid the compressibility problems which affected the Typhoon.

At low level the Tempest V could outrun any other piston-engined fighter. It entered service in April 1944 and was first used against V1 flying bombs. Its top speed of 670 km/h (416 mph) was attained at an altitude of 4,600 ft — 80 km/h (50 mph) faster than even the powerful P-47D at that height.

Thunderbolt was an excellent gun platform. With a 2,500 hp R-2800 the P-47D could achieve 685 km/h (425 mph); the experimental lightweight XP-47J touched 812 km/h (504 mph) with a 2,800 hp engine.

The fighters which won the Pacific war for the US Navy both used the same R-2800 engine as the Thunderbolt — the Chance Vought F4U Corsair and the Grumman F6F Hellcat. Both had six 0.5 in machine guns. The Hellcat was the more conventional design. The Corsair, however, had a distinctive cranked wing and a long nose which restricted vision for carrier landings, and only in April 1944 did it start operating from US carriers. Both were faster and more heavily armed than their Japanese adversaries: top speed of the Hellcat was 621 km/h (386 mph) while the Corsair could touch 685 km/h (425 mph). Hellcats built totalled 12,300, and the last of 10,500 Corsairs was not rolled out until December 1952.

The Soviet Union trailed behind the German and Allied industries as far as the design of airframes was concerned. Typical of Soviet fighters was the Yakovlev Yak-9, which entered service in August 1942. Although it could out-turn any of its opponents at low altitude, its speed was moderate at a maximum of 580 km/h (360 mph). Armament consisted of a single engine-mounted cannon (either a 20 mm ShVAK or a 37 mm Nudelman-Suranov) and a 0.5 in Beresin BS machine-gun.

Jets and rockets

Mid-1944 brought another shock for the Allies when, almost simultaneously, the Luftwaffe deployed the Messerschmitt Me163 rocket-powered intercepter and the Me262 twin-jet fighter-bomber.

The Me163 Komet has been described as the most dangerous aircraft ever ordered in quantity. Its fuel was a highly corrosive and volatile mixture

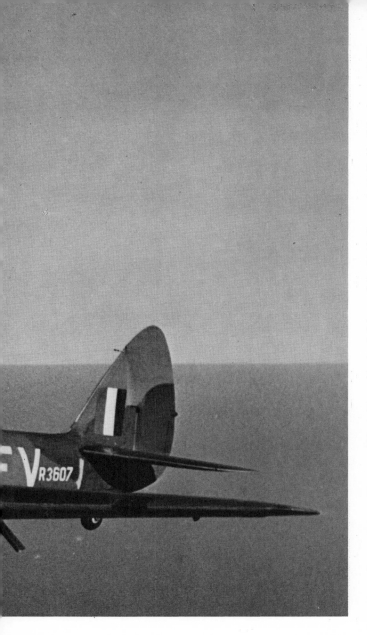

30 mm cannon. Powerplants were two Junkers Jumo 004B turbojets rated at 860 kg (1,900 lb) thrust. It was the slow delivery of these turbojets, rather than Hitler's insistence that the Me262 be modified as a fighter-bomber, which ensured that this advanced design had no significant effect on the course of the war.

Very few of the Me262s completed were issued to operational units. Potentially, it was a devastating intercepter with the speed to ignore the fighter escorts — one 45-aircraft unit, *Jagdgeschwader* 7, claimed to have destroyed 427 Allied aircraft between November 1944 and the end of the war.

The only other jet fighter to see action was the British Gloster Meteor. First flown in July 1943, the Meteor was a straight-winged aircraft substantially slower than the Me262: top speed of the fastest wartime variant, the Meteor III, was 794 km/h (493 mph), compared with the Me262's maximum of 870 km/h (540 mph). Early Meteor Is were used against V1 flying bombs in 1944, and a few Meteor IIIs were deployed in Belgium in April 1945.

Bombers

In no country was the relationship between bomber and airliner development closer than in Germany, banned from building combat aircraft under the Versailles Convention. Two of the bombers which took the offensive in 1939 had been designed five or six years earlier as dual-role aircraft: fast airliners for Lufthansa and bombers for the Luftwaffe.

The first of these, the Dornier Do17, was actually rejected for Lufthansa service because the accommodation offered to the ten passengers was impossibly uncomfortable. The slim profile of the Do17 earned it the nickname 'Flying Pencil' and helped it to an impressively high speed. When it was first flown in the autumn of 1934 it could outrun most fighters then flying, with a maximum speed of more than 385 km/h (240 mph). When it was rejected by Lufthansa its possibilities were recognised by the Luftwaffe, and a bomber prototype was ordered, this flying in the late summer of 1935. The Do17 bomber entered service with the Luftwaffe in early 1937 and was used in Spain by the Condor Legion. In its Do17P version it was one of the main Luftwaffe reconnaissance aircraft in the first two years of the war.

The other dual-role aircraft, the Heinkel He111, had a longer career than the smaller Dornier. It first flew in February 1935, but early bomber aircraft were seriously underpowered and service entry was delayed. The first production version was the

of 80 per cent hydrogen peroxide in water, with hydrazine hydrate and methyl alcohol as catalysts. If these fuels came into contact anywhere except inside the combustion chamber of the rocket motor the result was a devastating explosion. The Komet had no landing gear except a skid, and every touchdown was hazardous because of the risks of explosion if fuel lines were damaged in a heavy landing. Some 370 Komets were built, but they scored few successes because of the difficulty of hitting a slow bomber from a fast aircraft with the short-range MK 108 30 mm cannon. The Komet's climb rate — 2.6 min to 30,000 ft — was immeasurably faster than that of any other fighter of its day.

Even the 1,400 Me262s built could do no more than the Me163 to lengthen the war. The world's first operational jet fighter when it entered service in June 1944, the Me262 was an advanced design with swept wings, tricycle undercarriage, pressurized cockpit and a heavy armament of four

Above right A B-24 Liberator 'Betsy' of the 90th brigade, 5th AAF, on a mission to New Guinea, 24 February 1944.

Below right The de Havilland Mosquito Mk IV, an unarmed bomber carrying four 500 lb bombs internally; it was first used in May 1942.

He111B, with two Daimler-Benz DB600 engines. By the time war broke out in 1939 the He111B had been overtaken by new developments: the He111E with Junkers Jumo 211 engines; the He111F with a more angular wing which simplified manufacture; and the He111H, the main production version, with a new glazed nose replacing the conventional 'stepped' nose of earlier variants.

The He111H stayed in production longer than expected because of the failure of the aircraft which should have replaced it. By 1944, when production ended, 7,300 He11s had been built. The He111H-16 had two Jumo 211Fs of 1,350 hp and could carry a 2,000 kg (4,400 lb) bomb load. Defensive armament included a single 20 mm MG FF cannon and up to six machine-guns, all on hand-held flexible mounts. Range was 1,950 km (1,200 miles).

Of the war's British bombers the Fairey Battle had the shortest operational career. Designed as a long-range day bomber with a single Merlin of 1,030 hp, the Battle was neither fast enough to elude interception — with a top speed of 388 km/h (241 mph) — nor well enough armed to defend itself, with a single flexible-mounted machine-gun firing aft. The type was withdrawn to training duties following a few disastrous missions over France.

More successful was the Vickers Wellington, the second bomber to use the 'geodesic' system of construction, with fabric covering a 'basket-weave' metal framework. This gave the Wellington a remarkably light structure and its altitude performance was better than that of any other wartime British 'heavy'. Wellingtons were built with Bristol Pegasus (Wellington I), Rolls-Royce Merlin (Wellington II) or Bristol Hercules (Wellington III) engines. The Wellington X was powered by two 1,675 hp Hercules VIs and could carry an 1,810 kg (4,000 lb) bombload. Maximum speed was 411 km/h (255 mph) at 22,000 ft.

The Wellington served in a variety of roles other than bombing, including reconnaissance and minesweeping. For the latter mission it was fitted with a large magnetised 'hoop' braced to the fuselage and wings to detonate magnetic mines.

Like the German bombers, the Bristol Blenheim started out as a civil aircraft — the Bristol 142, commissioned by Lord Rothermere as a personal transport. When the military Blenheim entered service in March 1937 it was the world's fastest

72

bomber, with a top speed of 460 km/h (285 mph). Powerplants were two 840 hp Bristol Mercury radials. Blenheims were built in Canada as well as in Britain, under the name Bolingbroke.

The French aircraft industry only built 450 Lioré-et-Olivier LeO 451 bombers before the collapse of 1940, and those that did reach the squadrons were in many cases lost on tactical daylight missions for which the aircraft was not designed. One of the fastest bombers of its day, the elegant LeO 451 could touch 494 km/h (307 mph) on the power of two Gnome-Rhône 14N radials giving 1,140 hp each. Defensive armament included a 20 mm Hispano-Suiza HS-404 cannon in a dorsal position and a 7.5 mm MAC machine-gun in a retractable belly turret.

Masters-of-all-trades

Two of the most versatile aircraft of the war were designed as high-speed bombers and ended up performing nearly every role there was. The first to fly — in the Axis corner — was the Junkers Ju88 in December 1936. It was a twin-engined aircraft and followed normal German practice in that the crew was grouped in the nose, with hand-held guns rather than turrets. The bomb-bay was mainly intended for small weapons; heavier ordnance was carried under the wings. The aircraft was fitted with dive-brakes and was built to withstand the stresses of dive-bombing. Flaps spread over the entire span.

The Ju88 started to join the squadrons in September 1939. The first major production version was the Ju88A-4 bomber, powered by two Junkers Jumo 211J engines giving 1,350 hp. Up to 2,000 kg (4,400 lb) of bombs could be carried, and top speed was 470 km/h (292 mph). In 1940 a few Ju88C long-range fighters were delivered, with three 7.9 mm machine-guns and a 20 mm MG FF cannon in a solid nose. This led to the Ju88C-6B and Ju88R-1 night fighters (the latter with BMW 801 radials) fitted with the elaborate Lichtenstein radar arrays.

Production of fighter Ju88s overtook output of the original bomber in 1942 and moved on to the Ju88G. Late-production Ju88G-7s were armed with up to six 20 mm MG151 cannon and could attain 640 km/h (398 mph). Other variants of the Ju88 were used for reconnaissance and tank-busting, the latter version wielding a ventral 75 mm cannon.

But the classic multi-role warplane was the de Havilland Mosquito, the only bomber of the war which could safely dispense with defensive guns. The keys to its success were clean design, light-weight wooden construction and the high power available from later Rolls-Royce Merlin engines.

The first Mosquito prototype — a two-seat bomber — flew in November 1940. One year later the Mosquito B.IV bomber entered service, to be followed by the NF.II night fighter in May 1942. In the same month Mosquito bombers raided Cologne, and in January 1943 Mosquitoes bombed Berlin in daylight. From December 1943 the pressurized Mosquito B.XVI was in service, with a top speed of 668 km/h (415 mph) and a service ceiling of 40,000 ft. It was more than just a nuisance raider; it could carry an 1,800 kg (4,000 lb) bomb internally.

Night-fighter Mosquitoes with improved interception radar were used as 'intruders', harassing German night-fighter bases to take the pressure off Bomber Command. The FB.VI fighter-bomber, however, accounted for most of the 6,700 Mosquitoes built; it combined the four 20 mm cannon and four 0.303 in machine-guns of the fighter with an internal bomb-bay.

The Allied heavies

The bulk of the Allied air offensive, however, was carried out by the 'heavies' — big, slow four-

Above The Handley Page Halifax III, a four-engined heavy bomber, which shared with the Avro Lancaster most of the night offensive against occupied Europe.

Right The North American B-25 J20 Mitchell bomber, which carried a normal bomb load of 4000 lb and 13 0.5 inch guns.

engined aircraft with powerful defensive armament. The first to fly was the Boeing 299, built for a US Army Air Corps competition and flown in July 1935. But it was not until 1940 that production of the aircraft — by then known as the B-17 Flying Fortress — got into its stride. Early B-17Cs cruised at 37,000 ft on the power of four Wright R-1820 engines with exhaust-driven turbosuperchargers. A few, named Fortress Is, went to the RAF, who were unimpressed. Partly as a result of this experience, the B-17E was developed, with doubled defensive armament (12, as opposed to 6, 0.5 in machine-guns in powered turrets and flexible mountings). Power remained the same, at 1,200 hp per engine, so performance suffered. The later B-17G model added a 'chin' turret carrying two 0.5 in guns.

More Consolidated B-24 Liberators were built

than Fortresses (18,000 compared with 13,000) and it had a bigger bombload and longer range than the Boeing. It was a later design, first flexing its long, slender wing in December 1939, but it was never as popular with its crews as was the B-17, partly because it was nothing like so willing to stay in the air after taking battle damage. Like the Fortress, it had four 1,200 hp turbosupercharged radial engines (Pratt & Whitney R-1830s), and like the Fortress it gained a considerable amount of defensive artillery as the war progressed and fighter armament became heavier.

Britain concentrated on the night bomber, and the RAF used three main types of 'heavy'. First to enter service was the Short Stirling in August 1940. It was hampered by an official requirement that the wing span should be less than 30.5 m (100 ft) so that the new bomber could use existing hangars. Thus the Stirling's service ceiling was rather lower than that of the other two RAF bombers, and this put it at a disadvantage. Maximum bomb-load was 6,350 kg (14,000 lb) but the biggest single bomb that could be carried weighed 1,810 kg (4,000 lb) because of the design of the bomb bay. Like most British bombers, the Stirling defended itself with light machine-guns in powered turrets fitted in the nose and tail and beneath the fuselage. Later, a dorsal turret with two guns was added. The Stirling's power came from four 1,590 hp Bristol Hercules engines.

The Handley Page Halifax was the second of the night heavies, reaching the squadrons in November 1940. Early versions were underpowered, with four 1,280 hp Merlins; enterprising RAF squadrons stripped their aircraft of front and upper gun turrets and other items, reducing their losses despite the weaker armament. The Halifax III was an improved version; the front turret was replaced by a streamlined nose, and it had 1,615 hp Bristol Hercules XVI engines and extended wings.

But the most famous British bomber of the war was the result of an improvisation. In November 1940 the Avro Manchester twin-engined bomber entered service, but it was already clear that its 1,760 hp, 24-cylinder Rolls-Royce Vulture engines were never going to be reliable in service. Two months later, in January 1941, a derivative of the Manchester flew with four 1,480 hp Merlin XX engines. This was the first Lancaster.

The Lancaster had a better range and payload than the Halifax. Design bombload was 6,350 kg (14,000 lb), but later Lancasters carried a single 9,980 kg (22,000 lb) 'earthquake' bomb. Range with a more normal load was 3,780 km (2,530 miles). The standard defensive armament was eight 0.303 in guns in nose, tail and upper turrets.

Germany's strategic bomber

Meanwhile, the German heavy-bomber programme was in difficulties. In 1937 the German Air Ministry decided that Germany could not afford to start production of a four-engine bomber and should concentrate instead on easier-to-manufacture twin-motor machines. In the meantime, a very advanced bomber was to be developed and placed in production in 1941.

The Heinkel He177, which flew in November 1939, was a very sophisticated aircraft. Its two Daimler-Benz DB606 engines were formed of two DB601s coupled to a single propeller, and more

than 2,700 hp was promised. Fowler flaps which increased the area of the wing for take-off and landing were fitted over the entire span. But the aircraft was plagued with problems, including engine fires, and did not enter service until December 1942. By that time German command of the air was a thing of the past, and the He177 was rarely used in the heavy bombing role. It was used as an anti-shipping aircraft, armed with Hs293 or Fritz X radio-controlled glide bombs, but accident rates were always high.

Light attackers

The US industry built a total of 22,000 light twin-engine bombers during the war, backing up the heavy bombers. There were three main types. The Douglas A-20 Havoc was originally built as the DB-7 for the French, but the aircraft ordered were delivered to the RAF after the French surrender. The RAF used them for training and as night intruders. Later, more powerful versions were used by the USAAF as the A-20 bomber and P-70 night-fighter.

The second of the US twins, the North American B-25, won fame as the first US aircraft to raid Japan when 16 B-25s were flown off the USS *Hornet*. The B-25G and B-25H versions packed a 75 mm cannon in the nose for anti-shipping work, but accuracy was poor and the B-25J reverted to more conventional armament. The B-25H was one of the most heavily armed aircraft of the war, with 14 fifty-calibre machine guns, the 75 mm cannon and an assortment of bombs, rockets and torpedoes.

The Martin B-26 Marauder was a clean-looking aircraft, bigger and more powerful than either the A-20 or the B-25. Early versions were fast — up to 507 km/h (315 mph) on the 1,850 hp available from each of two Pratt & Whitney R-2800s — but the wing was small for the aircraft weight and landing speed was high. Consequently the Marauder was distrusted by its crews as a dangerous aircraft. But

it was the USAAF's main twin-engined bomber in Europe, and the RAF even used it as a long-range fighter on one occasion, when it wreaked havoc among unescorted Luftwaffe transports carrying relief supplies to North Africa.

Neither the Italians nor the Japanese produced bombers as effective as those of Germany and the Allies. The standard Italian bomber was the Savoia-Marchetti SM.79, unique among wartime bombers in having three engines. It was widely used for torpedo-bombing, for which the Regia Aeronautica pioneered the use of large aircraft.

Japan's most widely used bomber was the Mitsubishi G4M, code-named Betty by the US Navy. Flown in November 1939, it was a fast, clean aircraft, but throughout its career it was fatally deficient in armour and self-sealing fuel tanks, and it would often burn and crash under the withering fire of the American fighters' fifty-calibres. Like most Japanese aircraft it had an excellent range — some 5,600 km (3,700 miles). Towards the end of the war it was used as a mother ship for the Okha 11 rocket-powered suicide bomber.

Atomic bomber

The ultimate wartime 'heavy' was the Boeing B-29 Superfortress, which dropped the first atomic bombs on Hiroshima and Nagasaki and carried out the even more horrific napalm raid on Tokyo. Flown in September 1942, the B-29 incorporated many advanced features. It was pressurized so that the crew could be comfortable on long, high-altitude missions. The wing was long, slender and highly loaded, and was fitted with large area-increasing flaps. Instead of seating the defensive gunners inside the turrets, the B-29 used a complex system of remotely controlled 'barbettes' aimed with computing sights from within the fuselage. Defensive armament comprised twelve 0.5 in machine-guns and a 20 mm cannon in the tail.

The Superfortress was heavier and more powerful than any other wartime bomber. With four 2,430 hp, turbosupercharged Wright R-3350 radials its top speed was 576 km/h (358 mph) — fractionally slower than a 1940 Spitfire. Range with 9,100 kg (20,000 lb) of bombs was 5,230 km (3,250 miles).

From June 1944 the B-29s raided Japan from bases in China, but losses were high, due more to mechanical problems than to the efforts of the Imperial Japanese Air Force. The record improved

when the US forces took over the Marianas Islands bases in November 1944. In March 1945, however, all four of the defensive barbettes were removed and the B-29s, with their undersides painted black, switched from high-level day bombing to low-level night attack. Because of the high speed of the modified aircraft, fighters could only attack from the rear, so the B-29s kept their tail guns.

The war's only jet bomber

Only one jet bomber saw wartime service — the German Arado Ar234. First flown as early as June 1943 with a skid undercarriage and a trolley for take-off, the Arado was re-designed as the tricycle-gear Ar234B and entered service in the reconnaissance role in September 1944. No Allied fighter could touch the Ar234, with its 32,000 ft service ceiling and its 740 km/h (460 mph) top speed. As a bomber, with up to 1,500 kg (3,300 lb) of bombs beneath the fuselage and engine pods, it was equally hard to catch. It used two of the same Junkers Jumo 004B turbojets as the Me262 fighter, and like the fighter was usually a single-seater.

Attack aircraft

By the end of the Second World War a new class of aircraft was emerging, faster and nimbler than the bomber, but with a greater bomb-load and endurance than the fighter-bomber. The new class had its beginnings in the wartime dive-bombers, of which the most famous (or notorious) was the Junkers Ju87. Usually the Ju87 was known to its victims by the standard German abbreviation for Sturzkampfflugzeug (dive-bomber) — *Stuka*.

The Ju87 was an ugly aeroplane, but an eminently practical one. The cranked wing allowed a short undercarriage and good clearance for a heavy bomb load — up to 1,800 kg (4,000 lb) in later versions — and carried full-span flaps. The glasshouse canopy, perched high on the fuselage, gave an exceptionally good view. But at 410 km/h (255 mph) the Ju87's top speed was not enough to evade an attacking fighter, and the two flexibly mounted 7.9 mm guns in the rear cockpit were not enough to deter it. Once air superiority had been established, however, the Ju87 was a formidable bomber and later in the war, with two 37 mm cannon in underwing pods, a highly effective tank-buster.

Heavier armour than the Ju87 and a retractable undercarriage distinguished the Soviet Union's Ilyushin Il-2, possibly the most effective close-support aircraft of the war. Designed for level attacks with heavy cannon, rocket projectiles and bombs, rather than dive-bombing, the Il-2 was in

service right from the German invasion of Russia, from 1943 onwards in its more powerful Il-2m3 version with a rear gunner and defensive armament. Powerplant was one Mikulin AM-38F inline engine rated at 1,770 hp, and top speed at low level was 435 km/h (270 mph).

Carrier aircraft

Other wartime aircraft built for the attack role were carrier-based, such as the archaic but effective Fairey Swordfish. Despite its biplane layout and 224 km/h (139 mph) top speed it remained in production and under development until 1943, when the Swordfish III appeared with search radar and rocket or torpedo armament.

The Swordfish and the Skua dive-bomber were replaced aboard British carriers by a single type, continuing the trend towards fast, multi-role

Above A Fairey Swordfish over *Ark Royal;* these obsolete but tough aircraft did some notable work against the U-boats by dropping torpedoes.

Right A very successful seaplane, the Consolidated Catalina PBY. It was used at first for maritime reconnaissance and later for patrol-bombing.

'attack' aircraft. The Fairey Barracuda entered service in 1943. With its shoulder-mounted wing, massive flaps and mid-set tailplane it was no beauty, but it could carry a torpedo or a heavy load of bombs or rockets from the smallest escort carriers, often with the aid of booster rockets. Like the Swordfish it could carry ASV Mk X search radar. Powerplant was a 1,640 hp Merlin 32.

The US Navy used different types for the dive-bomber and torpedo roles throughout the war, although the multi-purpose Skyraider was under test in 1945. The dive-bomber which won the Battle of Midway was the Douglas Dauntless, developed from an original Northrop design and in service from 1941. It had an 1,800 km (1,115 miles) range and a crew of two. The Dauntless was supplemented and to some extent replaced by the Curtiss Helldiver, which carried its bomb load internally and had a more powerful Wright R-2600 engine. After a somewhat troubled development the Helldiver entered service in November 1943.

The Grumman Avenger torpedo-bomber was built in much larger numbers than either dive-bomber, some 10,000 Avengers being built by Grumman (as the TBF-1) and by General Motors (as the TBM-1 to TBM-3). It was unique among torpedo-bombers in that it carried its torpedo inside a bulky fuselage, and later it was used for rocket attacks. The Avenger's portly shape belied a 436 km/h (271 mph) top speed.

Maritime reconnaissance

The landplane and the flying boat shared the maritime reconnaissance role during the war; it was not until the late 1940s that the landplane came into the ascendant. First of the two most famous flying-boats of the war, the Consolidated Catalina, flew in 1935 as the XP3Y-1. Later its role was changed from patrol to patrol-bombing and it was redesignated PBY-1. The PBY served with RAF Coastal Command as the Catalina, and with the Soviet Navy as the GST. It was powered by two Pratt & Whitney R-1830s, and a high wing, carried on a slim braced pylon above the hull, gave it exceptional stability; it was said that the right way to turn a Catalina was to apply full aileron and sing three bars of *Anchors Away* before using the rudder. It was Catalinas which tracked the *Bismarck* during the chase which led to the destruction of the German battleship.

The RAF's main flying boat, however, was the Short Sunderland. Flown in October 1937, the Sunderland was a military version of the pre-war C-class boats built for Imperial Airways, with powered gun turrets in the nose and tail. Instead of carrying bombs externally or cutting a hole in the planing bottom of the hull, the designers of the Sunderland fitted it with bomb racks which could be winched out spanwise through doors in the fuselage side and underneath the high-mounted wing. The Luftwaffe called the Sunderland the *Stachelschwein* (porcupine) because of its ability to defend itself — one Sunderland emerged victorious from a running fight over the Atlantic with six Ju88 fighters. More than one Sunderland, holed and unseaworthy, made a successful landing on a grass airfield.

Between August 1940 and February 1941 one Luftwaffe unit, *Kampfgeschwader* 40, which seldom had more than eight aircraft serviceable at any one time, claimed to have sunk 363,000 tons of Allied shipping. The aircraft with which it was equipped was the Focke-Wulf Fw200C Kurier (Condor). Like the Sunderland the Kurier was derived from an airliner, the Fw200B; in fact, it was Japanese interest in a maritime-reconnaissance version which started development of the Fw200C, and the Luftwaffe only showed interest when it became clear that the Heinkel He177 was going to be later than planned. The Fw200C differed from the airliner in having a large ventral 'bathtub' fairing containing a bomb bay, with gun positions at either end. The Kuriers were more than a nuisance to Allied shipping, particularly as they worked in close co-operation with U-boats.

Transports

World War II was fought by air-mobile forces; the invasions of France in 1940 and 1944 were both

Left The British Short Sunderland Mk V flying boat, a capacious, reliable and long-ranged aircraft which continued in maritime service till 1959.

Above The Avro Lancaster, a powerful four-engined bomber, which could carry anything up to the 22,000 lb 'Grand Slam' bomb.

spearheaded by airborne groups. The Luftwaffe's standard transport was the Junkers Ju52 (affection-ately, *Tante Ju* or Auntie Ju), an elderly design even at the outbreak of war. It had three BMW 132 radials and the corrugated skin characteristic of Junkers designs in the early 1930s. It dropped paratroops over Norway, the Netherlands, the Balkans and Crete; it was fitted with a vast metal hoop under wings and fuselage to detonate mag-netic mines, and it operated as a floatplane.

But the most famous transport of the war years — and indeed of all time — was the Douglas DC-3 in its various versions. From the middle of 1942 Douglas concentrated on one basic military DC-3 with Twin Wasp engines, a large rear cargo door and a strengthened floor for freight, and nearly 10,000 of this version — C-47 to the USAAF and Dakota to the RAF — were built. It was built as the Lisunov Li-2 in the Soviet Union, and as the Showa L2D in Japan. It was tested, but not produced in quantity, as an amphibious floatplane. The USAAF even took the engines out of one C-47 and flew it as a glider.

Although the XCG-17 — the C-47 glider — had a better performance than most purpose-built gliders, it was probably too expensive. Purpose-built troop gliders like the Airspeed Horsa were one-shot machines, designed to pancake into any suitable field and unload troops, jeeps and guns. The Hamilcar was built to carry the specially designed Tetrarch light tank on airborne opera-tions. The vast Messerschmitt Me321 and Junkers Ju322 were designed to carry full-size tanks, but were too unwieldy to see service.

It has often been said that World War II spurred technical progress. But in the main — with the exception of some specialised fields such as radar — the war was fought and won largely with technology which had originated before 1939: the high-powered piston engine, turbosupercharging and pressurization. Advances such as the jet engine and the computing gunsight were used during the war, it is true. But the fact that there was a war on meant that they were pressed into service before they were properly developed; that had to wait for peacetime, and it was only after 1945 that really significant technological advances were made.

The Boeing B-29 bomber, which entered service in September 1942. The lower photograph illustrates its enormous size compared with other bombers of the time. It could demonstrate a range of 5380 miles and a maximum bomb-load of 20,000 lb.

Chapter 5
JET AGE-
MILITARY

THE immediate post-war period showed just how much the development of airframe structures, aerodynamics and systems depended on powerplants. The war years had seen the piston engine developed almost to its ultimate, and the propeller had begun to display limitations which would have to be overcome if performance was to reach the levels being demanded of the coming generation of combat aircraft. Propellers and reciprocating engines still have a part to play in military aviation, but the gas turbine proved to be the advance which revolutionised air warfare in all but the most basic departments.

The first jet fighters
The first jet aircraft to enter service in the world, the Gloster Meteor, had problems which held up development at the start. But, being larger than the first German jet aircraft, the Messerschmitt Me262, and having the distinct advantage of being

on the winning side, the British type proved more versatile in the end. Me262 development ceased at the end of the war, but this twin-jet fighter was nevertheless a remarkable aircraft. It was both faster and more heavily armed than the Meteor, and showed the way ahead in at least two respects. The 262's wing was slightly swept back to delay the increase in compressibility drag which occurs as the speed of sound is approached, and its two axial-flow Junkers Jumo turbojets were much more efficient than the Meteor's centrifugal-flow units.

What really started post-war development moving was the export of Britain's jet-engine technology to America, France, Sweden and, most significantly, the Soviet Union. The United States was the first to take full advantage, producing a whole array of new aircraft immediately after the war. They ranged from small fighters to giant bombers, all of them powered by US-built engines based largely on British ideas. Heading the parade

was the Lockheed P-80 (prototype for the F-80 Shooting Star, F-94 Starfire and the evergreen T-33 trainer), which flew for the first time on January 8, 1944, under the power of an imported de Havilland Goblin.

An Allison J33 was later substituted for the Goblin, and it was in this form that the Shooting Star became famous, playing a leading role in the early days of the Korean War and earning itself the distinction of shooting down the first aircraft in jet-to-jet combat. The victim was a Russian MiG-15 which, had it not been for the Rolls-Royce Nene engine, would almost certainly not have been there. The more powerful radar-equipped Starfire two-seater also did sterling work in Korea, particularly at night. But it was left to the North American F-86 Sabre to earn a place in the hall of fame by

establishing superiority over the MiG-15, which had surprised everyone with its ability to outclimb, out-turn and outrun everything put in its way.

Mikoyan and Gurevich (who formed the MiG bureau) had, like the Americans, benefited from German experience to produce the Fagot (as Nato code-named the MiG-15), a small, light, simple all-swept design which went on to be built in huge numbers. The F-86 was also all-swept and built round a British engine, the Wright J65 version of the Sapphire. By the beginning of the Korean conflict, the slats, extended wing leading edge and powered, all-flying tailplane surfaces of the E and F models allowed American pilots to overcome the generally superior climbing performance of the Russian type. Total production of the remarkable F-86 eventually ran to 9,500, more than any other Western military aircraft since the war. Development was extensive and included Navy versions powered by uprated J65s, Orenda-powered Canadian variants, and Australian CA-27s with the Rolls-Royce Avon 26. The F-86D, with radar in a modified nose section over the intake, was the first Sabre in which it was possible to carry out 'collision-course' interceptions, as opposed to the old-fashioned tailchase.

The Republic F-84 Thunderjet pipped the Sabre at the post to become the first aircraft to enter production for the US Army Air Force, as the USAF was then called. But the swept wing necessary for high speed was not applied to the F-84 until the F model, the Thunderstreak, which first flew in production form only in 1952. By then, straight wings were being discarded by virtually everyone. Sweden's Saab had put the first European swept-wing jet, the J29 Tunnan (nicknamed the 'Barrel'), into service the year before. In France, Marcel Dassault had produced the first of a series of aircraft which were to win him an enormous international reputation. The Ouragan, once again built round a licence-built Nene, was an extremely conventional, straight-wing design, but it led directly to the Mystère and Mirage fighter-bombers. The first Mystères were no more than Ouragans with 30°-swept wings, and it was a Mystère II powered by the first French jet engine, the axial-flow Atar, which became the first European aircraft to exceed the speed of sound.

Far left The North American F-86 Sabre gained its reputation against Russia's MiG-15 during the Korean War. Outgunned and in some respects outperformed, it eventually won overall superiority.

Top left Dassault responded to foreign customers' requirements for a relatively cheap but high-performance ground-attack aeroplane with the Mirage 5, a simplified version of the delta Mirage III.

Centre left The Tupolev Tu-95 Bear-D is an aircraft used for mid-course guidance of long-range Russian air-to-surface missiles. One is seen here being shadowed by an air-defence Phantom of the RAF.

Bottom left Latest in the line of light fighters from Northrop is the F-5E Tiger II, a higher-performance version of the T-38 Talon trainer and F-5A Freedom Fighter. In all, some 3,000 have been built.

Right Saab found the double-delta solution best answered its needs for power and performance in the relatively small airframe of the Draken. A J35F model of the Swedish Air Force is illustrated here.

Below right Two versions of the Dassault-Breguet/ Dornier Alpha Jet are being built, to meet the training and light ground-attack requirements of the French and West German Air Forces respectively.

Far right Only a moderate success in its native America, the Lockheed F-104 Starfighter has been a key weapon for European air forces such as those of Italy and West Germany, both of which built it under licence.

Britain, enjoying a head start in engine technology, had begun like everyone else with conservative aerodynamics — the unsuccessful Supermarine Attacker naval fighter-bomber and the enormously popular and long-lived Meteor both featured straight wings. The ubiquitous de Havilland Vampire (the most numerous post-war British type, with 4,206 built) was also conventional in its wing layout, and even relied on wooden construction and a modified version of the Mosquito's nose section for the side-by-side trainer variant. But prototypes of the ill-fated Supermarine Swift, the Scimitar (which had better luck with the Royal Navy) and the evergreen Hawker Hunter, all with swept wings, made their maiden flights in 1951.

Undoubtedly the most popular and successful post-war British fighter-bomber, the Hunter became a standard to rank with the Sabre and, later, the F-4 Phantom. Its combination of grace, handling qualities, reliability, strength and firepower make it a contender to be reckoned with even in the mid-1970s, when examples are still being refurbished by the manufacturer for resale to new customers. After a brief encounter with the Sapphire engine (fitted because it remained alight when the Aden cannon were being fired, unlike the Avon at first), the Hunter has always been powered by an unreheated Avon producing up to 4,500 kg (10,000 lb) of thrust.

At this time, one newcomer to the American

Above The Northrop F-89D Scorpion was one of the first big fighters to link an autopilot with its fire-control radar, thus allowing the aircraft to carry out automatic collision-course interceptions.

Left Though never operational, the North American X-15 was one of the most successful research aircraft of all time, and still holds the absolute world airspeed record at more than four times the speed of sound.

Above Labelled a fighter initially, the controversial General Dynamics F-111 has emerged as a most formidable medium-range, low-level bomber.

Right The USAF Vought A-7D Corsair II is one of the first tactical attack aircraft to combine inertial navigation and attack systems with a head-up display.

manufacturing scene was beginning to make a name for itself with the US Navy. Beginning with the Banshee, the McDonnell Aircraft Co was later to dominate US naval fighter-bomber development. After what was effectively a trial run with the FH-1 Phantom I, on the Banshee McDonnell stayed with a straight, laminar-flow wing and two Westinghouse J34 engines but added all-electric flaps, wing-folding and undercarriage systems. All-weather fighter-bomber versions followed the fighter originals, and by the time of Korea the Banshee family was ready to embark on an extensive and highly successful career during the conflict, operating night and day from USN carriers.

Flying alongside the Banshees were aircraft from another famous name in naval aviation. Grumman had flown a prototype F9F Panther, straight-winged and once again powered by a Pratt & Whitney-built Nene (known as the J42), in November 1947. The Panther was the first USN jet to take part in the Korean fighting, going on to bear the brunt of the carrier-based ground-attack work. The prototype F9F-6 Cougar, substantially the same as the Panther but with a completely new swept wing, flew in September 1951 and deliveries to the Navy began only two months later.

Intercontinental bombers

In the bomber field the world's manufacturers demonstrated some marked differences in approach. By far the most impressive, if for no other reason than its enormous size, was the Convair B-36. With an initial maximum loaded weight of 126,000 kg (278,000 lb) — a figure which eventually grew to over 181,440 kg (400,000 lb) in the B-36J — the B-36 was by far the largest aircraft ever to have approached production. It arose from a wartime requirement for a bomber capable, in the event of a British collapse, of flying from the United States to drop a heavy bomb-load on Germany. To achieve the payload-range required, the aircraft was powered by no fewer than six 3,500 hp Pratt & Whitney Wasp Major radial piston engines driving pusher propellers from installations buried in the trailing edge of the massively thick wing. They were supplemented by four General Electric J47 turbojets of 2,360 kg (5,200 lb) thrust each, pod-mounted in pairs three-quarters of the way along each 32 m (107 ft) wing. The prototype B-36 flew for the first time in August 1946 and the last of the 380-odd built was delivered in 1954. By then the production B-52 was already flying, and a good deal of the B-36's later career was spent in strategic reconnaissance.

In a wholly different mould was the Boeing B-47 Stratojet, which first took to the air on its thin, 35°-swept wings and six J47 turbojets (the first US axial-flow engines) in late 1947. With an internal bomb-load of nearly 10,000 kg (22,000 lb), a cruising speed of up to Mach 0.85, a range with bombs of more than 4,800 km (3,000 miles) and an advanced radar bombing system, the B-47 became the standard USAF Strategic Air Command medium bomber of the 1950s. It also appeared in electronic-countermeasures and reconnaissance versions.

Tactical bombers

In Europe, meanwhile, medium bombers of a different sort were in the pipeline. In Russia the first of more than 10,000 Ilyushin Il-28s flew in 1948, benefiting once again from Britain's donation of the Nene engine. Two of these Rolls-Royce powerplants, built in Russia as Klimov VK-1s, were used to power the Il-28 Beagle, which had straight, high-mounted wings and all-swept tail surfaces. Used as bombers, reconnaissance aircraft and trainers, Beagles remained in service with the Soviet Air Force up to 1970 or so, and are still in widespread use worldwide even now.

Britain's answer to post-war demands for such an aircraft proved to be another classic — the English Electric Canberra. Nearly 1,000 were made in Britain and Australia, plus another 400+ under licence in the United States. Designated B-57, most of the US Canberras were built by Martin and powered by J65 engines, but General Dynamics also turned out a number of extensively modified high-altitude reconnaissance versions fitted with TF33 turbofans. English Electric chief designer W. E. W. Petter deliberately chose a simple and elegant design which was not particularly advanced either in structure or aerodynamics. The two axial-flow engines were mounted centrally on the broad-chord, straight wings, giving excellent manoeuvrability and performance at both high and low altitude.

The original specification called for a high-speed, high-altitude radar bomber, but delays to the

Above left The great swept-wing Boeing B-47 Stratojet was a great technical advance in the 1940s and was the standard medium bomber for the USAF Strategic Air Command throughout the Cold War era.

Above Built for the strategic ranges and heavy bomb loads beyond the capabilities of the B-47, the Boeing B-52 Stratofortress was a landmark in big bombers.

Left The Venezuelan Air Force is but one of several South American and other countries to have bought, and still to operate, the magnificent and multiple-role English Electric (now BAC) Canberra.

The Handley Page Victor, designed as one of Britain's trio of V-bombers, has been developed into the RAF's standard air-refuelling tanker aircraft.

necessary advanced and reliable radar meant that early Canberras were 'visual' only, with the bomb-aimer sitting behind a glazed nose section similar to that of the contemporary Il-28. Two-seat trainer, photographic reconnaissance, target-marking and then ground-attack versions all followed, distinguished by nose-section and crew accommodation changes. The Mk 6 bomber featured integral wing fuel tanks and uprated engines, entering RAF service as a replacement for the earlier Mk 2 in 1954. The Canberra proved hugely versatile, also appearing in drone and target-tug versions, and acting as flying testbed for new engines and electronic equipment throughout the 1950s and 1960s.

The V-bombers
Britain also produced a remarkable run of aircraft designed to deliver nuclear weapons — the Valiant, Vulcan and Victor V-bombers. Required to build the Valiant in a hurry, Vickers-Armstrong resorted to comparatively low-risk technology and succeeded in flying a prototype in 1951. Transferred from high-altitude to low-level tasks in 1963, the Valiant immediately suffered severe fatigue problems and was withdrawn from service within a year. But it was the only one of the trio to fly in anger, attacking Egyptian airfields with high-explosive bombs during the Suez campaign of 1956.

Probably the meanest looking of the V-bombers was the Handley Page Victor. The last of the three to be built, the Victor embodied advanced light-alloy honeycomb construction, a T-tail, and a crescent wing which was thick and highly swept at the root and thinner and less swept at the tip. By this means Handley Page obtained the best possible handling over a wide range from approach speed up to the high-subsonic regime. But the technical achievements were overshadowed by delays in getting the Victor into service. Then, as the type's increasing vulnerability to interceptors and missiles at altitude became apparent, it was consigned first to the low-level role, in which it proved less successful than the Avro Vulcan, and then to air-to-air refuelling duties.

The delta-winged Vulcan was unique among the world's big bombers. It was also the only V-bomber to be designed to carry the Douglas Skybolt air-launched ballistic missile, later cancelled in favour of the Blue Steel stand-off bomb. Like the Victor, the Vulcan was eventually converted for strategic reconnaissance, a role which it still

performs. The RAF also deploys a number of Vulcans as low-level tactical-strike aircraft. Originally equipped with Avon and then Sapphire engines, the Vulcan was subsequently given four Rolls-Royce Olympus of 9,072 kg (20,000 lb) thrust. Thus powered by these exceptional engines, it displayed unmatched payload, range and altitude performance, especially when fitted with an increased-span, wider-chord wing and revised elevon controls.

Boeing's eight-jet Stratofortress
Compared with the 90,750 kg (200,000 lb) of the fully loaded Vulcan, America's mighty Boeing B-52 Stratofortress was a monster weighing roughly the same empty. Planned originally as a propeller-driven type, the swept-wing B-52 was made possible by the advent of the more efficient two-shaft Pratt & Whitney J57 turbojet originally developing 4,536 kg (10,000 lb) thrust. With most of the fuel in the wing, the eight-engined B-52B could carry 4,536 kg (10,000 lb) of bombs over 8,000 miles. But this was nothing compared to later models, which had completely 'wet' integral tank wings (B-52G) and more efficient and powerful turbofan engines (the B-52H with Pratt & Whitney TF33s).

The Stratofortress entered service in 1955, at about the same time as the Vulcan in Britain. It remains the standard strategic bomber of the USAF, with the peak number in service reaching well over 600 in the early 1960s. Like all long-lived aeroplanes, the B-52's navigation and weapon-aiming systems have been constantly updated over the years, and the B-52G and -H are now tasked with low-level penetration pending the arrival of the Rockwell B-1. The big Boeing will probably be best remembered for its 'carpet-bombing' activities in Vietnam and for the famous 'Linebacker' missions over the North, which eventually did as much as anything else to end America's involvement in the war.

Through the sound barrier
While the bombers were carrying more over greater ranges, fighters were beginning to go significantly faster. Basically subsonic types like the Hunter and Saab's Lansen were capable of exceeding the speed of sound in a shallow dive, but the first combat aircraft in the world to exceed Mach 1 in level flight was the North American F-100 Super Sabre. Powered by an afterburning J57, the F-100 was the first of the famous Century series of USAF fighters. With a 45°-swept wing of only 6 per cent thickness/chord ratio, the Super Sabre was unusual in having inboard ailerons, no flaps, and full-span leading-edge slats.

In 1954, shortly after its service debut, the F-100 had to be grounded when it was found to be prone to stability problems in the roll and yaw axes. But the solution to this new problem — which included the addition of wing span and fin height — did not hold up development for too long. The F-100 turned into a firm favourite with its operators (which included Denmark, France and Turkey), gaining a fine record both as fighter-bomber and top-cover fighter during the Vietnam war.

Following up the success of the MiG-15, Mikoyan produced the better-behaved Mig-17 Fresco before jumping on to the supersonic band-wagon with the MiG-19 Farmer. This type had a highly swept wing and twin afterburning engines. Large Fowler flaps and deep wing fences (to stop spanwise flow of the air and therefore loss of lift) guaranteed satisfactory low-speed handling. An all-moving tailplane later replaced the original fixed unit. Extreme manoeuvrability and the tremendous power of the 30 mm cannon made the Farmer a potent fighter, and it also entered large-scale production as the Shenyang F-6 in China. The first of an eventual total of 10,000 entered service in 1953, and the Farmer is still in use as a daytime fighter and limited all-weather intercepter armed with Alkali air-to-air missiles.

Above Designed in the very early 1950s, the Soviet MiG-19 was an outstanding fighter/interceptor and is still widely used, particularly by China.

Above right The North American F-100 Super Sabre was a natural successor to the F-86 and, after preliminary stability problems, proved a most successful fighter-bomber.

Contemporary with the MiG-19 was the American project for a single-seat supersonic all-weather intercepter which led to Convair's none too successful F-102 Delta Dagger. The company had flown the world's first true delta wing back in 1948, but the prototype Delta Dagger's drag proved very much higher than anticipated and the first F-102s never in fact exceeded Mach 1. The fuselage had to be redesigned to conform with the National Advisory Committee for Aeronautics' recently formulated area rule before Mach 1.25 could be achieved.

But the Delta Dagger showed the way as far as electronics were concerned, combining radar, computer and missiles in a semi-automatic system for the first time. It was not until the superficially similar but radically redesigned F-106 Delta Dart powered by the afterburning Pratt & Whitney J75 turbojet entered service in 1959 that USAF Air Defence Command got a true Mach 2-plus

intercepter with an automatic weapon system. Only now is a successor for the F-106 currently being sought in the long-running Improved Manned Intercepter programme.

While Convair was perfecting the F-106, McDonnell had produced its first aircraft for the US Air Force. The formidable F-101 Voodoo, which entered service in 1957, was big, with a maximum gross weight of around 22,680 kg (50,000 lb), and heavily armed with Falcon air-to-air guided missiles and Genie unguided nuclear rockets for the intercepter role, and with mines and conventional or nuclear bombs for attack. It was also endowed with an internal-fuel range of 2,400 km (1,500 miles) and a maximum speed of Mach 1.8 or more. Powered by two afterburning J57s of up to 6,800 kg (15,000 lb) thrust each, the F-101 resulted from a Strategic Air Command requirement for a long-range fighter-bomber escort. The type saw service with Tactical Air and Air Defence Commands in the USA, however, and the F-101F still serves as an all-weather intercepter with the Canadian Armed Forces.

The second half of the 1950s saw the emergence of a spate of delta designs. In 1955 Saab found that the double delta was the best way of packaging fuel and equipment in its Draken. Dassault experimented with swept and delta wings, and British and French engines, to arrive at the Mirage, a design which has probably done more for company and country than all the other Dassault types combined.

A Nato light strike fighter competition in 1953 saw Dassault proposing a swept-wing design which eventually became the French Navy's Etendard. But the French Air Force also needed a small intercepter, and for this Dassault proposed a delta powered by two Rolls-Royce Vipers and a liquid-propellant rocket booster. Operationally this came to nothing, but Dassault persevered and in 1956 flew the prototype Mirage III, an altogether larger delta-winged aircraft powered by a French engine, the Atar 101. In 1958 the Mirage IIIA prototype — incorporating bigger, thinner conical-camber wings and a new fuselage for the developed Atar 9 engine — hit the aviation headlines by becoming the first European aircraft to achieve Mach 2 in level flight. The French Air Force responded by ordering 100 of the Mirage IIIC intercepter version.

Since then Dassault has never looked back, selling vigorously abroad and enjoying an effective monopoly at home. From the IIIC were developed the two-seat trainer IIIB; the multi-mission, limited all-weather IIIE; the reconnaissance IIIR; and the Israeli-inspired Mirage 5, a day-only ground-attack version with simplified avionics and more fuel and weapon load. With an Atar 9 of about 6,125 kg (13,500 lb) thrust, the Mirage was regarded by the Israelis as underpowered. So, having a plentiful supply of General Electric J79 engines for their Phantoms, they decided in the late 1960s to re-engine the type with the 8,120 kg (17,900 lb) American powerplant. The technical difficulties were formidable, but the resulting Kfir and canard-equipped Kfir C2 will keep the Mirage shape prominent in the skies for many years to come.

After Korea the US armed forces began to call for higher-performance fighters and fighter-bombers. Ed Heinemann of Douglas came up with the almost unbelievable A-4 Skyhawk, a design small enough to be stored in aircraft carriers without having to fold its 'wet' delta wings, and yet able to carry a heavier-than-specified bomb load over a distance greater than that required. Early versions, weighing a mere 6,804 kg (15,000 lb), were powered by a single J65 but could still carry a 2,270 kg (5,000 lb) warload over a 740 km (400 nautical mile) radius of action. These days powered by a J52 of more than 4,990 kg (11,000 lb) thrust and weighing anything up to 12,300 kg (27,000 lb), the latest Skyhawks can carry a 4,082 kg (9,000 lb) weapon load and drop it with pinpoint accuracy

with the aid of advanced avionics which include a British head-up display. First delivered in 1956, the Skyhawk continues in production 20 years later, probably the longest run by any Western combat aircraft.

Russia's light fighter of the time, the MiG-21, is also a classic in its own right. The quest for greater performance resulted in an afterburning turbojet producing 4,990 kg (11,000 lb) of thrust to drive a thin-delta aircraft with swept tailplanes at speeds approaching Mach 2. The early models were day-only fighters, their endurance limited by a small fuel load and the comparative inefficiency of the single-shaft engine. But since then more fuel, better electronics and improved performance have been built in over a huge production run. The straightforward Fowler flaps of the first MiG-21s have been replaced by blown surfaces to reduce landing speed, and the new avionics make the type a useful, if still short-ranged, multi-purpose aircraft. The MiG-21PF, with a completely redesigned and enlarged nose inlet housing interception radar inside the shock cone, first

Below Perhaps the most remarkable light fighter-bomber ever built, Ed Heinemann's diminutive Douglas A-4 Skyhawk is still in production after over 20 years.

Right Multi-role combat aircraft for the 1970s and 1980s, Sweden's Saab 37 Viggen has to have short take-off and landing capabilities, hence the canard wing.

appeared in public at the Tushino display in 1961. The last fifteen years have seen this basic shape developed over hundreds of export aircraft.

Naval fighters and strike aircraft

Operations from heaving aircraft-carrier decks in ocean areas beyond reach of land bases impose demands which have resulted in some highly distinctive post-war aircraft. A wealth of fine US naval fighters and attack aircraft during the 1950s was matched in Britain by a cautious progression from the de Havilland Sea Venom (first flight in 1951) through the first Sir Sydney Camm jet fighter, the Hawker Sea Hawk, and the Supermarine Scimitar to the de Havilland Sea Vixen. An advanced, all-metal aircraft which first flew in 1951, the Sea Vixen was severely delayed by an accident at the Farnborough air show, and the Royal Navy had to wait until 1958 before getting its first missile-armed all-weather fighter-bomber.

In 1955 America's Vought company flew the F-8 Crusader, a Mach 1.6 fighter with a wing whose incidence could be increased by 7° for carrier operations. Bigger, heavier and carrying a great deal more fuel, the F-8 could nevertheless outperform the land-based F-100 on the thrust of the same J57 engine. This remarkable aircraft was subse-

quently developed into an all-weather fighter-bomber. Some 42 of these advanced Crusaders were sold to the French Navy, which armed them with R530 missiles in place of the Sidewinders or Bullpups of the US versions.

The Mach 2 fighters

While the F-8 was entering USN service, a radically different single-seat day intercepter was being delivered to USAF Air Defence Command. The Lockheed F-104A Starfighter was Clarence 'Kelly' Johnson's answer to the post-Korea call for more performance. This the Starfighter certainly had, boasting a Mach 2.2 maximum speed, an astonishing rate of climb and very high ceiling. Based on a single afterburning J79 engine and the smallest, thinnest wing yet seen, the 'manned missile' F-104A was under-armed, however, and did not see lengthy service.

But a Nato need for a tactical nuclear strike and reconnaissance type then transformed the Starfighter into a low-level attack aeroplane. In this guise it had a strengthened structure, manoeuvring flaps in place of the earlier blown surfaces, inertial navigation and multi-mode Nasarr radar. The move was a mixed blessing, providing European countries with their first taste of Mach 2

101

Left Russia's first strategic jet bomber, the Tupolev Tu-16 Badger, was originally a missile-carrier but is now largely used for various kinds of reconnaissance.

Right The Blackburn (now Hawker Siddeley) Buccaneer won late acceptance by the RAF, but is a formidable low-level tactical nuclear bomber.

performance, but forcing them to enjoy it on a type not originally designed for such a demanding job. Italy nevertheless proceeded with development of the European F-104G and in 1968 produced the F-104S. Featuring improved electronics and medium-range Sparrow air-to-air missiles, the F-104S is powered by the most powerful J79 variant.

But while most of the world's air forces were looking forward to getting a new generation of advanced equipment, Britain was in two minds. The 1957 Defence White Paper had announced blandly that manned combat aircraft were no longer needed, a statement which did more than a little to hinder the progress of British military aviation. Two notable projects were nevertheless continued: the English Electric Lightning (another Petter design) was the first supersonic all-weather fighter to enter RAF service, and the Blackburn Buccaneer turned into a formidable long-range, low-level naval and land-based attack aircraft. The Lightning had started life as a pure research project with no claims to operational usefulness and, as the P.1, had flown at Mach 1-plus back in 1954. A major redesign substituted afterburning Avons for the original unreheated Sapphires and replaced a two-shock intake with a central cone housing an intercept radar. The resulting P.1B exceeded Mach 2 in 1958 and was eventually cleared for service two years later.

With development held up in the wake of the 1957 White Paper, it was not until 1964 that more fuel, bigger engines and collision-course fire-control for the Red Top infra-red missiles were authorised. And only in 1965 did it prove possible to incorporate wing aerodynamic refinements which had first been flown on the research P.1 nine years before. The Lightning nevertheless climbs as fast as a Starfighter, manoeuvres a great deal better

than just about all of its contemporaries and, apart perhaps from the landing, has handling characteristics which have always delighted its pilots.

The most outstanding post-war heavy fighter of all, the McDonnell F-4 Phantom II, is a close contemporary of the Lightning. It began US Navy carrier trials as a long-range fleet-defence fighter in 1960, having flown in prototype form two years earlier. A two-seat, all-weather missile-carrier with Mach 2-plus performance, the Phantom was to be developed into a multi-mission fighter-bomber for sea and land operations. About 5,000 Phantoms have been sold so far, but the type was not without its early problems. It was once described as a 'triumph of thrust over aerodynamics', but the distinctive Phantom has since set many speed, height and rate-of-climb records.

Basic armament of the F-4's air-defence versions consists of infra-red Sidewinder and radar-homing Sparrow missiles, while the attack models can carry anything from rockets and iron bombs through precision-guided laser weapons to tactical nuclear bombs, up to a total weight of 7,250 kg (16,000 lb). The size of the aircraft, with a maximum gross weight of around 25,000 kg (55,000 lb), has been converted into operational flexibility: the Phantom is also used for reconnaissance, electronic warfare and surface-to-air missile suppression. Except for the Royal Air Force and Royal Navy aircraft, which are powered by the Rolls-Royce Spey, all Phantom variants have two afterburning J79 engines.

The Phantom is a classic example of the principle of product improvement. It has mounted at least seven different radars, for instance, the latest of which are pulse-Doppler units which can look down into ground 'clutter' in search of targets. The type has also been refined aerodynamically, with leading-edge slats being added to the F-4E and subsequent models during the 1970s in order to improve manoeuvrability. Operators other than the USN and USAF are almost too numerous to mention, but include the UK, Japan, Iran, Israel, Germany, Greece and Turkey.

The Soviet second generation

What had the Russians been up to since the mid-1950s? The conventional swept-wing Sukhoi Su-7 attack aircraft and Su-9 tailed-delta defensive fighter first appeared at a 1956 display. They were

clearly based on the same airframe and engine, a Lyulka AL-7F single-shaft powerplant developing 10,000 kg (22,000 lb) thrust. Similarly derived were the Su-11 with a large radar and new missiles, the Su-17 (introduced in about 1971) with its slatted swing-wings for improved field performance, and the Su-20 export version of the Su-17. It was not until about 1964 that Sukhoi flew the Su-15, a scaled-up version of the Su-11 with a very large nose radar and 'box' intakes for the two afterburning Tumansky turbojets. A vehicle for Anab infra-red and radar-guided air-to-air missiles, the Su-15 Flagon entered service in 1969 and is still in production.

Russian aircraft are notable more for their longevity than for their advanced technology, a tendency most marked in Soviet bomber development. The Tupolev Tu-16 Badger, which entered service in 1954, depended heavily on technology derived from the Boeing B-29, built in Russia as the Tu-4. Designed as a strategic bomber with two wing-root-mounted turbojets delivering 9,070 kg (20,000 lb) thrust each, it is best known as a launcher of Kennel and Kipper stand-off missiles, and as a maritime surveillance and electronic countermeasures aircraft. Its successor, the Tu-20 Bear, is also a missile launcher and multiple-purpose reconnaissance/ECM aircraft. Twice as large as the Badger, the Bear has huge swept wings with integral fuel tanks and four Kuznetsov turbo-props producing nearly 15,000 hp each and driving contra-rotating propellers. Both types are still in service.

Supersonic bombers

The laurels for producing the first supersonic bomber in the world went to Convair and the B-58 Hustler, though Tupolev and his more conservative Tu-22 Blinder were not more than a couple of years behind. The slim, delta-winged Hustler (which first flew in 1956) had four podded under-wing J79 engines and a huge weapon and fuel pod beneath the fuselage, and was made largely from stainless-steel honeycomb. Although the technical problems of Mach 2 flight with an aircraft of this size — gross weight was over 72,575 kg (160,000 lb) — were largely overcome, the Hustler cannot be counted a major operational success. The few that were built were all retired with fatigue problems in 1970 after only ten years' service.

North American flew its astonishing A-5 Vigilante in August 1958, introducing all at one go a host of aerodynamic and electronic advances which were almost all to become standard over the ensuing years. At a gross weight of 42,880 kg (80,000 lb), the Vigilante was the biggest and most

Right Competing strongly in world markets with the Alpha Jet, Hawker Siddeley's Hawk is being delivered as a trainer to the Royal Air Force and should win wider acceptance as a trainer/light attack aircraft.

Below right The Lockheed T-33 has been the world's major jet trainer for many years, only now being replaced by newer types. It was based on the F-80 Shooting Star single-seat fighter-bomber.

Far right The Lockheed C-130 Hercules is by far the best known and most popular post-World War II Western transport, several sub-variants having also been developed for special military and civil duties.

complex aircraft ever to operate from a carrier deck. It had large, blown flaps giving a low approach speed, with differentially operated slab tailplanes and a slab fin for low-speed control. The A-5's automatically scheduled variable-wedge inlets and nozzles were designed to get the best possible response from the two J79 engines over a very wide speed range. When another 6,800 kg (15,000 lb) of fuel capacity was built in, boundary-layer control had to be added to full-span leading-edge wing droop to maintain lift at low speeds. At the heart of this complex airframe lay the most advanced radar, inertial navigation and weapon-aiming systems. Capable of cruising at Mach 2 and more than 65,000 ft, the Vigilante turned reconnaissance aircraft in 1962, after the USN relinquished its carrier-based strategic nuclear role. Now designated the RA-5C, it is equipped with multiple sensors, including sideways-looking radar, and performs a vital role in naval and military recon-

naissance based aboard many of the larger USN carriers.

Jet and turboprop transports

There have been few significant military jet transports, and almost all of them have been American-built. Probably the most important of all was the Boeing C-135/KC-135, first flown in civilian guise as the Model 367-80 in 1954. Without the business represented by the 800-odd C-135s which were built, Boeing might never have raised the development money necessary for the enormously successful civil 707 programme. Well over 20 different transport, tanker/transport, VIP, electronic intelligence/countermeasures and research versions of the C-135 have been built. Early models were powered by J57 turbojet engines, while later versions have the more efficient TF33 turbofan engines. The computer-packed E-3A Airborne Warning and Control System (Awacs) still uses the

same basic airframe.

It was not until the Lockheed C-141 Starlifter, which first flew in December 1963, that another specialised strategic transport was built. The C-141 has a lower cruising speed than the C-135 but is capable of lifting heavy and awkward loads out of smaller airfields. It also boasts a rear loading door and ramp, a feature pioneered by the same manufacturer ten years earlier on the still-selling C-130 Hercules.

The 'Herc', with its four Allison T56 turboprop engines and pressurized fuselage, has undergone comprehensive improvement over the years to emerge as a virtually unbeatable battlefield tactical transport. More than 1,400 Hercules have been sold all over the world, as many as the Soviet Union's Antonov An-12. Similar in concept and capability, the An-12 can carry a 20,000 kg (44,000 lb) payload over 3,200 km (2,000 miles). The McDonnell Douglas YC-15 and Boeing YC-14

short take-off and landing jet transports are currently contending to replace the Hercules as a transport aircraft.

While the Soviet Union has elected to stay with turboprops for its vast An-22 strategic freighter — only going to turbojets for the Il-76 Candid first flown in March 1971 — the USA opted for advanced high-bypass-ratio General Electric TF39 turbofans for the Lockheed C-5A Galaxy. The first flight took place on June 30, 1968. Although structurally deficient (virtually the whole wing is having to be replaced to bring fatigue life up to specification) and unable to carry the originally required 56,700 kg (125,000 lb) payload over 12,875 km (8,000 miles), the Galaxy is in a class of its own when it comes to carrying outsize cargo. The C-5A has already proved its outstanding capability by making possible the speedy and successful airlift of American arms and equipment to Israel during the October 1973 war.

The sub-hunters

The requirements for surveillance and reconnaissance aircraft are enormously varied. Typical of the post-war tendency to develop maritime surveillance and anti-submarine aircraft from civilian airliners is the Lockheed P-3 Orion, a much-changed turboprop Electra which can 'stooge' for ten or more hours using acoustic and electronic sensors to seek out submarines. The latest P-3C variant is highly automated, containing a digital computer with a 458,000-word memory. Even more remarkable for its electronic miniaturisation and packaging is the carrier-borne Lockheed S-3A Viking anti-submarine aircraft, which has as much electronic capacity in an airframe less than half as big as the Orion's.

Mach 3 and variable geometry

Also destined for the recce business was the Lockheed A-11, YF-12 and SR-71 series, dreamt up as a U-2 replacement in Kelly Johnson's 'Skunk works' and flown for the first time in 1962. Powered by two Pratt & Whitney J58 turbo-ramjets each giving 14,750 kg (32,500 lb), the A-11 was the first aircraft capable of sustained Mach 3 performance, cruising at 80,000 ft or more. The YF-12A was a one-time contender for the Improved Manned Intercepter programme, equipped with radar, infra-red sensors and long-range missiles in an internal bay. But only the SR-71 strategic reconnaissance aircraft has survived in operational form. This extremely advanced aircraft is made of a titanium alloy and requires special high-temperature fuel.

Russia's closest equivalent of the A-11 series is the MiG-25 Foxbat. Not as advanced structurally, being largely made of steel, the Foxbat has been built in intercepter and high-altitude reconnais-

sance versions and is capable of short periods of Mach 3 flight. Superficially similar to the McDonnell Douglas F-15, the Foxbat is not a high-energy fighter in the same mould, relying instead on large Acrid air-to-air missiles and a radar with performance similar to that of the unit fitted to the Phantom. Its significance lies mainly in the fact that it was breaking speed and rate-of-climb records in 1965 and 1967, about ten years before the Americans began putting the F-14 and F-15 into full-scale service.

The ever-increasing need to build flexibility into complex and extremely expensive combat aircraft resulted in 1964 in what was supposed to be a multi-purpose fighter-bomber for both the US Air Force and Navy, the General Dynamics F-111. It was the first variable-sweep aircraft to enter service, but unfortunately the requirements initially proved over-ambitious. The new Pratt & Whitney TF30 turboshaft engines were plagued with development problems, the airframe was severely overweight, there were structural failures and the advanced systems did not work as they should have done. These difficulties were eventually overcome (even though the USN cancelled its F-111B fighter order) and the 45,000 kg (100,000 lb) attack versions have proved their worth as highly accurate, deep-penetrating bombers.

Variable geometry has remained very attractive in spite of the F-111's vicissitudes. It has been selected for three significant Western aircraft, and for the multi-role MiG-23 Flogger, the Su-19 Fencer (the first modern Soviet fighter to be developed specifically as a fighter-bomber for the ground attack role) and the new Backfire strategic bomber. In the West, Grumman put the swing-wing F-14 Tomcat into USN service in 1972. Despite TF30 engine problems and substantial cost increases, the F-14 is without doubt the most capable intercepter/fighter ever built. Apart from the variable-sweep wings, which are automatically scheduled to move to the right angle for the prevailing Mach numbers, the Tomcat airframe contains a number of components made from such light, strong, advanced materials as boron epoxy. The Hughes AWG-9 radar and fire-control system is the most powerful ever put into a combat aircraft. It can track as many as 24 targets while still looking for more, decide which ones constitute the greatest threat, and then fire off up to six Phoenix air-to-air

missiles almost simultaneously. The Phoenix has a proven effective range of over 100 miles, but if it should fail, the Tomcat can resort to Sparrow medium-range missiles and dogfighting Sidewinders. If after all that an adversary is within close range, the Tomcat pilot can exploit manoeuvrability born of a very high power-to-weight ratio and automatic wing sweep to bring the 20 mm Vulcan cannon to bear.

The biggest of the variable-geometry aircraft, flying in prototype form since December 1973, is the Rockwell International B-1 bomber. Designed to replace the B-52 in the 1980s, the B-1 can carry at least four times the destructive firepower of the big Boeing, mainly in the form of up to 24 Short-Range Attack Missiles (Sram) on rotary launchers in its three huge internal weapons bays. The B-1 is designed to penetrate enemy territory at low level and very high subsonic speed. Like the F-111, it carries an automatic terrain-following radar.

Also capable of low-level penetration and equipped with terrain-following radar is the much smaller Panavia Tornado multi-role combat aircraft (MRCA), the third of the Western variable-

geometry types. It is remarkable not least for the fact that it is designed and built by Britain, Germany and Italy to meet the differing requirements of the three air forces and the German Navy. This it will do with only two major variations on the same airframe and highly advanced Turbo-Union RB.199 three-shaft afterburning turbofan engines. The so-called common Interdictor-Strike (IDS) Tornado, to be delivered to all four services from about 1979, can carry up to 8,000 kg (18,000 lb) of weapons out of a maximum gross weight of less than 22,500 kg (50,000 lb). It will also be able to deliver them extremely accurately, thanks to a very advanced digital navigation and weapon-aiming system. The other version, for the RAF only, is called the Air-Defence Variant (ADV). It differs from the IDS mainly in having increased fuel capacity, by virtue of a small fuselage stretch, and a totally different radar which emphasises the air-to-air role and is linked with the Hawker Siddeley Dynamics 'snap-up/snap-down' Sky Flash development of the Sparrow missile. The Tornado will be the first aircraft in the world to enter service with a full 'fly-by-wire' control

system. This weight-saving technique replaces traditional mechanical control linkages with wires which carry electrical signals from the pilot's control column and rudder pedals.

Variable-sweep wings help shorten take-off and landing runs, important if roads and the like are used for runways in wartime. This the Swedish Air Force plans to do, but its Saab Viggen uses another formula — a delta mainplane and a canard foreplane with flaps.

Dogfighters for the 1980s

The outstandingly well equipped Viggen was unfortunate in 1975 to lose a potential order from Belgium, the Netherlands, Norway and Denmark to the General Dynamics F-16, perhaps the flashiest fighter for years. The F-16 combines most known methods of obtaining extreme dogfighting manoeuvrability, notably a thrust-to-weight ratio of better than one-to-one. It also features light, non-metal structures and reduced stability margins, which can now be exploited by means of fly-by-wire technology. These control-configured vehicle (CCV) techniques are being pioneered in the General Dynamics type mainly because it emerged from a flight-test programme designed to demonstrate this form of technology. The F-16 has still to prove itself operationally, but as a lightly armed, clear-weather fighter it will undoubtedly take some beating for years to come.

The F-16 is small, having a fighter-mission gross weight of about 10,450 kg (23,000 lb), and is

Above With huge swinging wings, the Mach 2 Rockwell B-1 bomber will be smaller than a B-52 but will be able to carry a heavier payload at low level.

Right Latest of the new, glamorous fighters, the General Dynamics F-16 is very manoeuvrable — this is partly because of its very high thrust-to-weight ratio.

powered by a single Pratt & Whitney F100 afterburning turbofan producing about 10,900 kg (24,000 lb) of thrust. This engine was developed specially for the outstanding big land-based fighter of the 1970s, the McDonnell Douglas F-15 Eagle. The F-15 is powered by two F100s at a typical mission gross weight of just over 18,100 kg (40,000 lb). Primary armament is the 'snap-up/snap-down' Sparrow and, like the Tomcat's AWG-9, the Hughes APG-63 pulse-Doppler radar is highly automated. The Eagle, with a range on internal fuel of more than 1,600 km (1,000 miles), is an uncompromised air-superiority fighter. Its high thrust-to-weight ratio and large conical-camber wing make it capable of outmanoeuvring just about anything else in the skies. Exceptions are the F-16 and, under certain conditions, the AV-8A.

Vertical take-off: the unique Harrier

AV-8A is the designation given by the US Marine Corps to possibly the most significant military aircraft since the day the jet engine made long concrete runways necessary — the vertical take-off Hawker Siddeley Harrier. The Harrier, developed as the P.1127 in a company private venture, is built

around the unique Rolls-Royce Pegasus high-bypass-ratio vectored-thrust turbofan engine. Cold air from the Pegasus fan and hot air from the core of the engine are ejected through two pairs of swivelling nozzles which direct the thrust directly down, forwards or even backwards. Like all the best ideas it is essentially simple, but solving the problems of control and payload-range called for years of development.

The P.1127 first flew in October 1960, but it was not until 1969 that the RAF received its first operational aircraft. In that time, engine thrust had been virtually doubled to 8,600 kg (19,000 lb). Power has since been further increased to 9,750 kg (21,500 lb) to allow a useful load of fuel and weapons to be carried over an acceptable distance after a short or vertical take-off. Thrust clearly has to exceed weight for a vertical take-off, so the

Harrier automatically starts out with an advantage as a dogfighter. The thrust-vectoring nozzles can be swivelled downwards while the aircraft is still in forward flight to rapidly dump speed or tighten up a turn. Fully developed, such VIFF (vectoring in forward flight) techniques could make the Harrier unbeatable in a close-in fight.

Today's development effort is concentrated on two main areas. Weight is generally the most critical parameter in Vtol aircraft design. US licensee McDonnell Douglas is therefore planning a lighter, composite-material wing and a range of high-lift devices for the new AV-8B for the US Marine Corps. Secondly, Vtol combat aircraft are tremendously valuable to navies with usable decks, large or small. This the British Government has recognized, and the first 'navalized' Sea Harrier is due to fly in late 1977.

Chapter 6
JET AGE–
CIVIL

D URING the war, air transport had been confined to the operation of essential services. In most places passengers had to have very good reasons for making a journey, and often needed government permission to fly. In the United States the airlines maintained a large route network for essential travel, a service kept in operation almost entirely by the twin-engined Douglas DC-3.

When World War II ended the US airlines urgently required new aircraft, as did the airlines of Europe, Australia and some other nations. In addition, many countries wanted either to expand their airline operations or, in many cases, to form new airlines.

Demobbed airliners
The DC-3 — known initially as the DST (Douglas Sleeper Transport) — went into service in 1936, subsequently being adopted by the US military

The Vickers Vanguard, a turboprop airliner, which first went into service with BEA in 1961.

forces and supplied to America's allies. A total of 10,655 examples of all versions was produced in the United States, and the type had also been built in Japan and turned out under licence in the Soviet Union as the PS-84, later redesignated Li-2.

At the end of the war there were very large numbers of surplus military DC-3s (by then generally known as Dakotas). These aircraft became the main equipment of most of the world's airlines, and several hundred are still in service with minor operators. One DC-3 is known to have flown more than 84,000 hours.

Two larger four-engined aircraft had been designed in the United States and ordered by the airlines during the war. But when they came off the production lines they were impressed into military service and denied to the airlines until the end of the war. These were the Douglas DC-4, which went into military service as the C-54 Skymaster, and the Lockheed Constellation. DC-4s were built in large numbers, and after the war surplus military examples were made available to airlines in the US and elsewhere. In addition, 79 were built after the war as civil aircraft. Only about a score of Constellations had been produced for military service, and all of them were subsequently converted to civil aircraft. Final Constellation production amounted to 233.

In wartime Britain priority was given to the construction of operational aircraft, but a number of Lancaster bombers were converted into Lancastrian transports. The Lancaster was also developed into the York transport, produced initially for RAF service but later released to BOAC. York production was stepped up in 1945 and the type gave many years of useful if extremely noisy service.

Germany had built transport aircraft during the

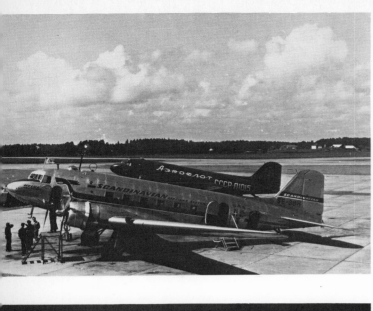

ance, supplemented the DC-4 and entered service with airlines such as Air-India International. In spite of early problems the Constellation was an outstanding aeroplane, with a beautifully shaped fuselage and triple fins and rudders. Its great advantage over the DC-4 was its pressurized cabin and, cruising at up to 480 km/h (300 mph), it was about 160 km/h (100 mph) faster.

The Brabazon Committee

In Europe little could be done during the war to prepare for peacetime air transport. But the British Government realized that new transport aircraft would be urgently required and, in December 1942, set up the Brabazon Committee to make recommendations for the development of post-war transport aircraft. The resulting recommendations covered nine types. Type I was a non-stop North Atlantic aeroplane. Production of the resulting design, the Bristol 167 Brabazon, ended with only one prototype completed. Type IIA, a short-haul piston-engined aeroplane for British and European airlines, emerged as the Airspeed Ambassador, a few of which were built for BEA. The Type IIB requirement produced a contrasting pair: the short-haul turboprop Vickers-Armstrongs Viscount, of which over 400 were built, and the Armstrong Whitworth Apollo, which ran to only two prototypes. Type IIIA was a medium/long-haul Empire-route aircraft. The result, the Avro 693 project, was cancelled. The Avro Tudor II was developed as an interim type to fill in before the arrival of the new designs, but was put forward as the Type IIIB by the second Brabazon Committee. Type IV, a North Atlantic turbojet type, evolved into the de Havilland Comet 1. Type VA, a piston-engined feederliner, became the Miles Marathon, only a few of which were built. Type VB, a small piston-engined aircraft for light-traffic routes, resulted in well over 500 de Havilland Doves.

Joining the Avro Tudor as interim types were the Vickers Viking, Bristol 170 Freighter/Wayfarer and Handley Page Hermes. Transport flying-boats also continued in production.

war, mostly the three-engined Junkers Ju52/3m. Also built in France and Spain, the Ju52/3m had been widely used by the airlines in pre-war years and some remained in service for several years after the war. They served at that time with DNL Norwegian Air Lines, and SAS subsequently used floatplane versions on Norwegian coastal routes. Some captured examples were used for a short time by BEA on British domestic routes.

American Overseas Airlines, Pan American Airways and TWA all used DC-4s on North Atlantic services. The type worked the US transcontinental routes, was widely adopted by European airlines, and operated on trunk routes in many parts of the world, including Australia, South Africa and South America. Thus in the second half of the 1940s the principal airliners in service were the mainly 21-seat DC-3 and the DC-4 with 40 or more seats.

Constellations, originally of about the same capacity as the DC-4 but with superior perform-

As the Brabazon recommendations show, there was a post-war need for a variety of transport aeroplanes. One was for what was regarded as the DC-3 replacement; much effort went into designing such an aeroplane, but no single type ever succeeded in replacing it, nor could perform exactly the same tasks as the ageing Douglas.

The search for a DC-3 replacement

The Viking was the British answer. It first flew in June 1945 and entered service with BEA in August 1946. Based on the Wellington bomber, the Viking was powered by two 1,675/1,690 hp Bristol Hercules engines, had a cruising speed of a little over 320 km/h (200 mph), and could originally accommodate 24–27 passengers in an unpressurized fuselage. It served for several years as the main equipment of BEA, as well as being operated by airlines in many parts of the world. Some 163 Vikings were built.

In the United States there were two main contenders for DC-3 replacement orders: the Convair CV-240 and the Martin 2-0-2. These were twin-engined monoplanes with nosewheel under-carriages, and both were powered by 2,400 hp Pratt & Whitney R-2800 engines. The most successful was the 40-passenger, pressurized CV-240, which entered service in June 1948 with American Airlines. Numerous airlines ordered the CV-240 and 176 civil examples were built. The CV-240 led to the improved 44-passenger CV-340 of 1952, and finally to the still further improved CV-440 Metropolitan of 1956. Eventually more than a thousand civil and military Convair-Liners were built, 240 of which were modified to take Allison or Rolls-Royce Dart turboprops. Thus powered, they were designated CV-580s, 600s and 640s.

The unpressurized Martin 2-0-2 entered service as a 42-seater in 1947 with Northwest Airlines in

Below A Convair CV-880 of Japan Airlines. Neither this nor the 990 model were successful commercially.

Above right A Convair CV-990A of the Spanish airline Spantax. This aircraft was one of the first to have turbofan engines.

Below right One of BEA's fleet of de Havilland Comet 4Bs. They went into service in October 1958, after the tragic failure of the Comet 1.

the USA and LAN in Chile. The type suffered a number of serious accidents and was withdrawn from service, but after some strengthening and re-engining returned to service in 1950 as the Martin 2-0-2A. Only 45 Martin 2-0-2s and 2-0-2As were built, but an improved version, the 48/52-seat pressurized 4-0-4, went into service with TWA in October 1951 and was also adopted by Eastern Air Lines. Including the prototype and two aircraft for the US Coast Guard, there were 104 Martin 4-0-4s.

The Soviet Union, too, urgently needed a postwar short-haul transport. This was met by the Ilyushin Il-12, which can best be described as a cross between a Viking and a Convair-Liner. The Il-12 was powered by two 1,650/1,775 hp Shvetsov ASh-82FN engines, initially had seats for about 27 passengers, and cruised at 350 km/h (217 mph). The type first flew in 1946 and entered passenger service with the Soviet airline Aeroflot on August 22, 1947. Large numbers were built for civil and military service and some were supplied to CSA, the Czechoslovak airline, LOT, the Polish airline, and to CAAC in China.

The Il-14, an improved version of the Il-12 with uprated engines and increased capacity, flew in 1953 and the Il-14P (Passenger) version went into service with Aeroflot at the end of November 1954. Very large numbers of civil and military Il-14s were built, some of them in East Germany and Czechoslovakia, and many are still in service.

Above One of the Fokker F.27 Friendships operated by Air Congo, now renamed Air Zaire. It is a 40/52 seater for short/medium range traffic, and typical of the medium-sized airliners of the 1960s.

Right BOAC's first Bristol Britannia 312, outside the Brabazon hangar at Filton, Bristol. This was an economical turboprop-powered aircraft which went into service in December 1957.

One other aircraft in this category was the Swedish Saab Scandia, which first flew at the end of 1946. It had seats for 32 passengers, was powered by two 1,800 hp Pratt & Whitney R-2180 engines and cruised at 340 km/h (211 mph). Only 18 (some built by Fokker in the Netherlands) went into service with SAS in Europe and VASP in Brazil.

Although the Viking gave many years' good service, few of Britain's early post-war transport aircraft were very successful. The four-engined Avro Tudor appeared in several versions and the Tudor 4 went into service on mid-Atlantic routes with British South American Airways; but two disappeared en route and BOAC never operated those it had ordered. Probably the best work done by Tudors was the carriage of fuel during the Berlin Airlift. The similar Handley Page Hermes was more successful: BOAC operated a fleet of Hermes 4s, mainly on African routes, from 1950 until the end of 1955, after which they served with a number of independent airlines. The Hastings military version of the Hermes 1 gave prolonged service to the RAF.

The interim Yorks and Lancastrians did well enough, but they were noisy and uneconomic and, although Lancastrians did make possible a 63-hour service between England and Australia, they were certainly not in the same class as the American aircraft of the period.

Bristol's Type 170 was an unusual aeroplane. Unlike most of the other aircraft of the time it was a high-wing monoplane with a non-retractable undercarriage. It was powered by two Bristol Hercules engines and had a large-capacity box-like fuselage. Of the 200 or so built for civil and military use, a few were Wayfarer passenger aircraft but most were Freighters with double nose doors. One of the best-known operations by Bristol Freighters was the cross-Channel vehicle ferry service of Silver City Airways, on which they carried cars in the main hold and had passenger cabins aft. For many years the type also operated cargo ferry services between New Zealand's North and South Islands. A higher-capacity Superfreighter with lengthened fuselage was specially designed for cross-Channel services.

Another high-wing monoplane, but of much cleaner design, was the pressurized 47/49-passenger Airspeed Ambassador, introduced as the *Elizabethan* class by BEA in March 1952. Twenty were operated out of the 23 built, but BEA was the only customer. They did however see service with several airlines after being disposed of by BEA.

The first post-war French aeroplane to go into

airline service was a four-engined type, the SNCASE SE 161 Languedoc. This was the pre-war Bloch 161 design which actually made its first flight in September 1939 but did not go into production until after the war. It was a low-wing monoplane with twin fins and retractable under-carriage, and was originally arranged to carry 33 passengers. Of the 100 built, Air France began using a number between Paris and Algiers in May 1946, and others saw service with Air Liban, LOT, Aviaco in Spain, Misrair in Egypt and several North African airlines. Gnome Rhône engines were originally fitted but most had Pratt & Whitney R-1830s.

The early post-war Italian airlines employed a number of three-engined Fiat G.12s and G.212s and four-engined Savoia Marchetti S.M.95s, but these were wartime designs or their developments and were of no special significance.

America sets the pace

The real advances in transport aircraft design took place in the United States, where Douglas developed the DC-4 into the DC-6 and DC-7 series and Lockheed produced the L.1049 Super Con-stellation and finally the L.1649. The DC-6 was an enlarged and pressurized development of the DC-4. It had four 2,400 hp Pratt & Whitney R-2800 engines and accommodation for 50 passengers, cruised at 450 km/h (280 mph) and entered service with American Airlines and United Air Lines in April 1946, cutting the eastbound transcontinental journey time to about 10 hours. DC-6s were operated by several airlines and more than 170 were built. Next came the DC-6A and DC-6B, with longer fuselages and greater range. The DC-6A was a cargo aircraft used mainly by the US Air Force and Navy, but the DC-6B proved to be one of the world's outstanding transport aeroplanes. Some 288 were built, the first going into service on American Airlines' transcontinental route in April 1951. The DC-6B began life as a 54-passenger aeroplane but later carried as many as 102 people.

In Montreal, Canadair built developments of the DC-4 and DC-6 powered by Rolls-Royce Merlin liquid-cooled engines. Although extremely noisy and, in the first version, unpressurized, the Canadair Four gave good service to Trans-Canada Air Lines as the North Star and to BOAC as the Argonaut.

Left One of BEA's fleet of Hawker Siddeley Trident 3s, now operated by British Airways. It has proved very successful on short-haul routes.

Below The prototype Vickers-Armstrong VC10 in BOAC livery. This is a long-range civil transport featuring rear-mounted engines.

Bottom A McDonnell Douglas DC-10-30 of the French airline UTA. This wide-bodied jet came into service in 1971, soon after the original 'jumbo jet'.

The Super Constellation went into service with Eastern Air Lines at the end of 1951. Really a Constellation with a fuselage 5.47 m (18 ft) longer and 2,700 hp Wright Cyclone engines, it accommodated between 66 and 102 passengers.

Production of the 3,400 hp Wright Turbo-Compound engine enabled Douglas and Lockheed to further improve their designs. Douglas produced the DC-7, capable of regularly flying non-stop across the United States in 8 hours eastbound and 8¾ hours westbound. It had accommodation for 60-95 passengers and entered service in November

Top An Air France Sud-Aviation Caravelle I, the first rear-engined airliner.

Above A British Caledonian Airways BAC One-Eleven.

Top right The famous Dash 80 prototype Boeing 707.

Above right The turbojet airliner Tupolev Tu-134 introduced into service with Aeroflot in 1967.

1953. Four United States airlines ordered the DC-7, and 110 were built. Then came the longer-range DC-7B, of which 108 were built for US airlines, plus four for South African Airways. The ultimate DC-7 was the slightly bigger, 60/105-seat

DC-7C with North Atlantic non-stop range. This was designed for Pan American and entered service as the Seven Seas in June 1956. The last Douglas piston-engined airliner, the DC-7C ran to 121 examples.

The Super Constellation also underwent steady development through the L.1049D and E up to the final G (passenger) and H (cargo) models. The last two versions were capable of carrying streamlined wingtip fuel tanks to give a range of well over 6,400 km (4,000 miles). More than 600 Super Constellations were built and they saw worldwide service for

many years until superseded by the first generation of jet airliners.

Finding that the DC-7C was superior to the Super Constellation in range, Lockheed decided to make their type competitive by designing a completely new one-piece wing spanning 45.7 m (150 ft). The resulting aeroplane was the L.1649A Starliner, which could carry up to 99 passengers and had a maximum-fuel range of more than 9,600 km (6,000 miles). But the L.1649A appeared too late and only 43 were built, with Air France, Lufthansa and TWA as the only customers.

Another United States type which deserves mention is the Boeing Stratocruiser, developed from the Boeing B-50 bomber via the C-97 military transport. The Stratocruiser was a large aeroplane with a wing of 43 m (141 ft 3 in) span and an initial maximum weight of 61,363 kg (135,000 lb). It used the same wing, tail unit and engine installation as the B-50 but had a new double-deck, double-lobe pressurized fuselage with seats for 55-100 on the main deck and a lounge and cargo holds on the lower deck. The engines, four 3,500 hp Pratt & Whitney R-4360 Double Wasps, gave a lot of trouble and earned the Stratocruiser a reputation for unreliability. But passengers liked the aeroplane and crews appreciated its spacious flight deck and superb view. The Stratocruiser first flew in July 1947, and Pan American ordered 20 of the 55 built and put them on North Atlantic services in 1949. The type was also bought by American Overseas Airlines, BOAC, Northwest Airlines and United Air Lines. Stratocruisers were particularly popular on the BOAC and Pan American North Atlantic first-class services, and many people

Above A Boeing 727 of Royal Nepal Airlines. This is a short/medium range airliner with three rear-mounted engines.

Right One of Indian airlines fleet of Boeing 737s, a short-haul version of the 727 with wing-mounted twin engines.

regretted their replacement by less comfortable jet aircraft in 1958.

One other double-deck landplane saw airline service. This was the French Breguet 763 Deux-Ponts. Studies for the design began in 1944 and the production version entered service with Air France on routes linking France with North Africa in March 1953 under the class name *Provence*. The mid-wing monoplane Deux-Ponts was powered by four 2,100/2,400 hp Pratt & Whitney R-2800 engines and had triple fins and twin rudders. Within the very deep fuselage the upper deck had accommodation for 59 tourist-class passengers and the lower deck had space for 48 second-class passengers or cargo. The large rear loading doors

Right One of Air France's Boeing 747F cargo aircraft with its nose loading door raised. This special freighter version of the 747 is now in service with a large number of cargo operators.

Far right above A Boeing 747B of South African Airways ready for take-off on a night flight. This photograph illustrates the graceful lines of the aircraft, despite its enormous size.

Far right below One of Eastern Airlines Lockheed L.1011 TriStars. It is powered by the advanced technology RB.211 turbofan engine developed by Rolls-Royce, and has been in service since April 1972.

in the underside of the fuselage were used for embarking vehicles when Air France had 6 of its fleet of 12 converted to Universal freighters. Civil operations ceased in March 1971.

The turbine era

Britain and Germany both had jet aircraft in service at the end of the Second World War. After the war Germany was forbidden to operate aircraft, but in Britain the potential of turbine power for civil aircraft had been fully realized. Development took place in two directions: the turbojet or straight jet which propels the aircraft with high-speed exhaust gases, and the propeller-turbine (or turboprop), in which the turbine is used to drive an orthodox airscrew or propeller.

British manufacturers developed designs employing both systems. These were the pure-jet de Havilland Comet and the propeller-turbine Vickers-Armstrongs Viscount and Armstrong Whitworth Apollo. The Apollo was not a success; there were only two prototypes and it requires no further mention.

The prototype Viscount V.630 made its first flight on July 16, 1948; the first Comet made its maiden flight on July 27, 1949, just beating the Canadian Avro C-102 Jetliner, to take its place as the first jet transport to fly. The Avro appeared only in prototype form, and although it achieved over 800 km/h (500 mph) the project was cancelled.

The Viscount was a 32-passenger low-wing monoplane powered by four slender Rolls-Royce

The Concorde was the first supersonic transport to enter into regular passenger service. It commenced operations on 21 January 1976.

Dart engines. Cruising speed was 440 km/h (276 mph) and range 2,200 km (1,380 miles). On July 29, 1950, the Viscount prototype began two weeks of operations on the London-Paris route with BEA — the first passenger services ever operated by a turbine-powered aircraft. Following the Paris flights, the Viscount was used briefly on the London-Edinburgh route during that year's Edinburgh Festival. But the V.630 Viscount was regarded as too small for economic operations and was therefore developed into the enlarged and more powerful V.700 series.

The Viscount 700 series did not go into service until 1953. As a result, it was the Comet 1 which became the first turbine-powered aeroplane to go into regular airline service. The Comet was a beautiful aeroplane with a slender circular-section pressurized fuselage and sweptback wing leading edge. Its four de Havilland Ghost turbojets, developing 2,020 kg (4,450 lb) thrust each, were buried in the wing roots and two cabins provided seating for 36 passengers. Cruising speed was 788 km/h (490 mph) and cruising altitude up to 40,000 ft but its range was limited to 2,800 km (1,750 miles). Flying in the Comet was a completely new experience: it flew at higher altitudes and cut flight times by approximately half. BOAC introduced this aircraft on its London-Johannesburg route on May 2, 1952, when it covered the 10,760 km (6,724 miles) in less than 24 hours.

Comets were subsequently introduced on the routes to Pakistan, India, Ceylon, Singapore and Tokyo, and Air France and the French airline UAT also put them into service. But then, on the first anniversary of the start of Comet operations, one broke up in flight near Calcutta, followed by a second in January 1954 near Elba. The type was grounded, but after investigations and modifications the Comet returned to service on March 23, 1954. On 8 April disaster struck a third time near Naples, and the type was finally withdrawn from service. The official accident report stated that the pressure cabins failed due to fatigue as a result of the pressurization and depressurization cycles.

From that time there were no turbojet transports in service until Aeroflot introduced its first jet, the Tupolev Tu-104, in September 1956.

By the time the Comet was withdrawn, the turboprop Viscount 700 was fully established in service, having begun regular operations with BEA on the London-Rome-Athens-Nicosia route on April 18, 1953, and on London-Rome-Athens-Istanbul the following day.

Like the Comet, the Viscount established a new standard of air travel. It was quiet, had low vibration levels, was fast and had magnificent large oval windows providing superb views. It was adopted by airlines all over the world, was the first major British transport aeroplane to be adopted by an American carrier, and became the first British aeroplane to be bought by China when six were ordered by CAAC.

Several versions of the Viscount were produced during a production run of 445, and wherever the type was introduced traffic rapidly increased, in some cases by more than 100 per cent. Until BEA introduced jet aircraft the Viscount served most of its routes. BEA's successor, British Airways

Above Concorde was simultaneously launched by British Airways and Air France.

Above right *Clipper Bald Eagle* was one of Pan American World Airways' Douglas DC-7Cs.

128

European Division, still has a fleet of 70-seat V.802s and V806s, and apart from other duties they operate most of the airline's Scottish services.

First of the thousands

On July 15, 1954, an important event took place at Seattle in Washington State — the first flight of a yellow-and-brown four-jet transport prototype known as the Boeing 367-80. This much loved aeroplane, normally referred to as the Dash 80, was the prototype Boeing 707, the United States' first jet transport. This large aeroplane, with wings swept back at 35° and four turbojets housed in pods mounted on pylons below and forward of the wing, combined the proven features of the B-47 and B-52 jet bombers. Boeing was to sell more than 3,000 commercial jet transports by mid-1976.

The first order for the Boeing 707 was placed by Pan American, and the first production aeroplane, the 707-120, made its first flight on December 20, 1957. The 707-120 was generally similar to the Dash 80 but slightly larger. It was powered by four Pratt & Whitney JT3C turbojets of 5,625 kg (12,500 lb) thrust, had a span of 39.9 m (130 ft 10 in), weighed 116,818 kg (257,000 lb) fully loaded, could carry up to 179 passengers, cruised at 912 km/h (570 mph) and had a maximum-payload range of 4,920 km (3,075 miles) without fuel reserves. The type entered service between New York and Paris on October 26, 1958. The Boeing 707 was considerably bigger and heavier than any other civil transport then in service and it set the pattern for the modern transport aeroplane.

Boeing built numerous variations on the original design, including the 707-220 with increased power to meet the specific needs of Braniff International Airways, and the short-body 707-138 to meet the requirements of Qantas.

The Boeing 707 was an impressive aeroplane but the early models did not have North Atlantic non-stop capability. Accordingly, the Model 120 was followed in 1959 by the 189-seat Model 320 Intercontinental. This version was designed for trans-ocean operations, was powered by JT4A engines giving 7,180 kg (15,800 lb) thrust, and had a maximum weight of 141,820 kg (312,000 lb). The Boeing 707 sold worldwide, and by May 1962 more than 170 had been delivered. A few customers, including BOAC, Lufthansa and Air-India, opted for the Model 420 with Rolls-Royce Conway bypass engines of 7,955 kg (17,500 lb) thrust.

The introduction of the Pratt & Whitney JT3D turbofan offered improved performance and fuel economy, and Boeing powered the 707-320B passenger and 707-320C cargo aircraft with this improved engine. Many of the earlier aircraft were re-engined with the JT3D and the suffix B was

added to their type designations. Boeing also produced the short-body Models 720 and 720B. By the end of August 1976 a total of 919 Model 707s and 720s had been ordered, of which 905 had been delivered. In service with 127 operators, these aircraft had flown 21,760 million km (13,600 million miles) and carried more than 516 million passengers.

The second jet transport was the Douglas DC-8, a design broadly similar to the Boeing 707 which first flew in May 1958 and entered service with Delta Air Lines and United Air Lines on September 18, 1959. The DC-8 had approximately the same dimensions, weights, capacity and performance as the Boeing, and the first version, the Series 10, was powered by four Pratt & Whitney JT3C turbojets giving 6,135 kg (13,500 lb) thrust. The first model was followed by the Series 20 with JT4As, and then came the JT4A-powered long-range Series 30, the Rolls-Royce Conway-powered Series 40, and the JT3D turbofan-powered Series 50. A cargo version with large side door was the DC-8-50F Jet Trader. Further development led to the Series 60, which appeared in three versions: the DC-8-61 of 1966, with an 11.27 m (37 ft) increase in fuselage length and accommodation for up to 259 passengers; the DC-8-62, with a slight increase in length and span and up to 189 seats; and the DC-8-63 of 1967, with the -61 long fuselage and -62 larger wing. Maximum seating in the -63 was 269 and maximum take-off weight 159,090 kg (350,000 lb). Production of the DC-8 ceased early in 1972 after 556 aircraft had been completed.

Comet reborn

Following the disasters to the Comet 1, de Havilland had been working on a successor. This was the Comet 4 with longer fuselage, four Rolls-Royce

Above The Mainliner
Stratocruiser *Hawaii* was
one of United Air Lines' fleet
of Boeing Stratocruisers.
The Stratocruiser was
Boeing's first commercial
airliner after World War II.

Right A Tasman Empire
Airways Lockheed Electra.
This view shows that most of
the wing was in the propeller
slipstream. The turboprop
Electra first entered
commercial service in 1959.

The long-range propjets

Strange as it may seem in retrospect, two large British propeller-turbine transports entered service at the beginning of the jet era. BOAC wanted a medium-range aeroplane for what were called the Empire routes. This was conceived as a piston-engined aeroplane but redesigned for turbine power. The aircraft was the Bristol Britannia, powered by four Bristol Proteus turboprops and produced in two main versions: the Series 100 for medium-stage routes, and the Series 300 for long stages. The prototype first flew in August 1952, but its development was prolonged and the 90-seat Britannia 100 only entered service in February 1957 when BOAC introduced it on the London-Johannesburg route. The Britannia 300, with accommodation for up to 139 passengers, entered service in December 1957, when it operated the first turbine-powered air services across the North Atlantic. But the Britannia appeared far too late and only 85 were built, including 23 for the RAF. Later the type was developed mainly for cargo use as the Canadair CL-44.

The other type was the Vickers Vanguard, which first flew in January 1959. This was a large aeroplane accommodating up to 139 passengers on the main deck and offering ample cargo capacity on the lower deck. The engines were four 4,985/5,545 hp Rolls-Royce Tynes, the loaded weight was 64,090 kg (141,000 lb), and the cruising speed exceeded 640 km/h (400 mph). Only 43 Vanguards were built, all for BEA and Trans-Canada Air Lines, and the type did not enter service until the winter of 1960. Some of the BEA aircraft were later converted to all-cargo Merchantmen.

Similar to the Vanguard but somewhat smaller and more commercially successful was the Lockheed Electra powered by four Allison turboprops. This California-built 66/99-seat aircraft, with a range of 4,458 km (2,770 miles) at 652 km/h (405 mph), entered service in January 1959. But a rash of structural failures, though successfully diagnosed and cured, put an end to new orders, restricting total Electra production to just over 170.

Convair late-comers

In addition to the Boeing 707 and Douglas DC-8 there were two other US first-generation jet transports: the Convair (later General Dynamics) CV-880 and CV-990. In appearance they followed the Boeing and Douglas layout but were smaller and faster. They were short/medium-range aircraft with five-abreast seating for a maximum of 130 passengers in the CV-880 and 158 in the CV-990, and each had four General Electric engines. The CV-990 was unique in having four shock bodies — looking rather like inverted canoes — extending

Avon turbojets giving 4,762 kg (10,500 lb) thrust, and accommodation for 60-81 passengers. The new Comet first flew in April 1958, and on October 4, 1958, BOAC operated the first-ever jet services across the North Atlantic when two Comets flew inaugural east and westbound services on the London-New York route. BOAC operated a fleet of 19 Comet 4s. In 1960 BEA also became a Comet operator when it introduced the Comet 4B with reduced span, lengthened fuselage and seating for up to 101 passengers. In the same year a third version, the Comet 4C, entered service. This combined the wing of the Comet 4 with the fuselage of the Comet 4B. This new family of Comets was ordered by several airlines and the RAF, and 75 were built.

behind the wing. These 'Küchemann carrots', as they were known in recognition of the German aerodynamicist, were fitted for aerodynamic reasons but in practice were used to carry additional fuel. The CV-880 was designed to meet TWA requirements but first entered service with Delta Air Lines in May 1960. The CV-990 was designed for American Airlines and began service with that airline and, as the Coronado, with Swissair in March 1962. Development delays restricted production to 65 CV-880s and 37 CV-990s.

Europe's tailjets

Britain also produced large jet transports, but with very limited sales success. First came the Vickers VC10 designed for BOAC and flown for the first time in June 1962. It had four Rolls-Royce Conway bypass engines mounted in pairs each side of the rear fuselage, keeping the wing unobstructed and ensuring outstanding take-off and landing performance. The large tailplane was mounted on top of the vertical fin in what is known as the T-tail configuration. Maximum seating was for 151. The VC10 began service with BOAC on the London-Lagos route in April 1964. Longer by 3.96 m (13 ft) and 10,455 kg (23,000 lb) heavier at 152,272 kg

Above RMA Robert Falcon Scott was one of British European Airways first Vickers-Armstrong's Viscount V.700s.

Above right A Boeing 720B. The 720 was designed as a smaller version of the long range Model 320 Intercontinental. The 720 first flew in 1959.

(335,000 lb), the Super VC10 version, seating a maximum of 174, was introduced on North Atlantic services in 1965. These aircraft were very popular with passengers but appeared too late. Only 54 were built, of which 14 went to the RAF.

One of the most successful European jet transports was the French Sud-Aviation Caravelle, designed to meet a 1951 specification for a medium-range transport. It was a very clean low-wing monoplane, novel in that its two turbojets were mounted one each side of the rear fuselage — a pattern that was to be followed by many later designs for transports and executive aircraft. The original Caravelles were powered by Rolls-Royce Avons of 4,762 kg (10,500 lb) thrust, had accommodation for up to 80 passengers and cruised at 740 km/h (460 mph). The first prototype flew on May 27, 1955, and production Caravelle Is entered service with Air France and SAS in May 1959. Several versions were produced, the final Caravelle

12B being capable of carrying 128 passengers, and Caravelles were used in many parts of the world, including the United States. About 280 were built.

In Britain BEA had a requirement for a medium-range transport, and in the United States Boeing decided that there was a need for a similar aircraft. In general the two resulting designs appeared remarkably alike. The British Trident, designed by de Havilland and produced by its Hawker Siddeley successor, was a low-wing monoplane with three rear-mounted engines and T-tail. The later Boeing 727 had the same configuration. The Trident 1, powered by three Rolls-Royce Spey engines of 4,477 kg (9,850 lb) thrust and seating 96 passengers, first flew in January 1962 and entered service with BEA in the spring of 1964. The type made a major contribution to the development of automatic landing for passenger services, the first of which was made by a Trident in June 1965. Subsequent models were the 1E, 2, 2E and 3, the last-named having accommodation for up to 179 passengers and being powered by three Speys of 5,422 kg (11,930 lb) thrust, plus one tail-mounted Rolls-Royce RB.162 booster engine delivering 2,385 kg (5,250 lb). A total of 117 Tridents have been built, including 35 for China's airline CAAC.

The prolific 727

The Boeing 727, with accommodation for 86-131 passengers and powered by JT8Ds of 6,350 kg (14,000 lb) thrust, made its first flight in February 1963 and entered service a year later with Eastern Air Lines and United Air Lines. The aircraft has undergone continuous development and as the Advanced Model 200 has engines each giving 7,257 kg (16,000 lb), carries up to 189 passengers and has a maximum take-off weight of 94,318 kg (207,500 lb), compared with the original aeroplane's 72,570 kg (160,000 lb). The Boeing 727 is by far the best-selling jet transport — by the end of August 1976, 1,305 had been ordered and 1,213 delivered. The type had then flown 14,681 million km (9,176 million miles) and carried more than 850 million passengers.

In spite of the multiplicity of jet transports at the beginning of the 1960s, there was still believed to be a market for about 1,000 80-seater twin-jet short/medium-range aircraft. The British Aircraft Corporation was first in the field with the BAC One-Eleven, which had rear-mounted Spey engines and accommodation for up to 89 passengers. The first flight took place in August 1963, but the prototype was lost in an accident and the programme slipped. As a result, the One-Eleven

did not enter service until April 1965, by which time Douglas had flown its similar DC-9. Entering service at the end of that year, the original DC-9 had accommodation for up to 90 passengers and was powered by JT8D turbofans.

Sales of the DC-9 soon overtook those of the BAC One-Eleven, mainly because Douglas made available the -30 model seating up to 115 passengers. The One-Eleven and DC-9 have now been produced in a number of versions, and by mid-1976 BAC had sold 220 aircraft and Douglas more than 850.

One other aeroplane was built in this category — the Boeing 737 with two wing-mounted JT8D engines and accommodation for up to 99 passengers. Although its fuselage was relatively short, the 737 retained the cross-section of all the previous Boeing jet transports. The first aircraft flew in April 1967 and the type went into service in the spring of 1968. Like the other Boeings, the 737 has been developed into an entire family of aircraft and 489 had been sold by the autumn of 1976.

Turbine short-haulers

Although the pure-jet aeroplane had proved its ability to operate economically over a wide variety of routes, there was still a place for the turboprop types. Four of these need to be mentioned. Britain

Above The Fokker F.28 Fellowship is the successor to the F.27. It is fitted with two rear-mounted Spey engines and entered service in 1969.

Right The YS-11 was the first Japanese plane to be exported. The picture shows a YS-11 operated by Olympic Airways of Greece.

and the Netherlands both built similar high-wing monoplanes, each powered by two Rolls-Royce Darts and capable of carrying about 50 passengers. The British type was the Handley Page Dart Herald, which first flew in March 1958 and entered service in May 1961. The Dutch aeroplane was the Fokker F.27 Friendship, which flew in November 1955 and entered service in September 1958. The F.27 was also built in the United States by Fairchild, and it was one of these American aircraft which first went into airline service. Only 48 Heralds were completed, but the Fokker is still in production and orders exceed 650.

The third aircraft in this group is the low-wing Hawker Siddeley (Avro) 748. It too is powered by two Dart engines, and has very good airfield performance. The HS.748 first flew in June 1960, entered service in 1962 and is still in production. Civil and military sales exceed 300 and about 50 have been built in India.

Bigger than the British and Dutch aircraft is the

Japanese YS-11, a 46/60-seat aircraft powered by two 3,060 hp Dart engines. This went into service in Japan in 1965 and more than 120 were built. The YS-11 was the first Japanese aeroplane to find overseas markets, with numbers exported to the USA, Canada, South America, Greece and the Philippines.

In May 1967 Fokker (by then amalgamated with Germany's VFW) flew a jet successor and supplement to the F.27. The new aircraft, with two rear-mounted Spey engines, was the F.28 Fellowship. Designed to operate from short, rough runways, the aircraft went into service in March 1969. More than 100 have been sold and there are several versions. Because of its low noise level the F.28 is the only jet aircraft allowed to operate from Stockholm's Bromma Airport.

Being sold in parallel with the F.28 is the VFW 614 short-range type, with 40-44 seats and two overwing-mounted Rolls-Royce/Snecma M45H engines of 3,527 kg (7,760 lb) thrust. The VFW 614 entered service in 1975 and so far has been sold in small numbers.

The wide-bodies
During the 1960s passenger traffic was doubling every five years and air cargo was growing even faster. Airports and airways were becoming congested, presenting the airlines and airport authorities with serious problems. But the availability of the 40,000-50,000 lb (20-25 tonne) turbofans meant that much bigger aircraft could be built to handle the explosive growth in traffic, at the same time reducing the number of airport movements.

The first and biggest of the new aircraft was the Boeing 747, which had twice the power, weight and capacity of its predecessors. The 747 is a vast aeroplane with a wide, two-aisle fuselage accommodating an average of 360 seats, and more than 500 in some versions. An upper level houses the flight deck and a lounge, and beneath the main deck there is cargo capacity equal to that of an all-cargo Boeing 707. The 747 went into service in January 1970 at a maximum weight of 323,635 kg (712,000 lb), and the latest versions can operate at 372,727 kg (820,000 lb). Span of the 747 is 59.63 m (195 ft 8 in). More than 300 747s have been ordered in several versions, including a nose-loading freighter and the short-body 747SP. The latter has a range of more than 6,000 miles (9,600 km).

Next appeared two very similar wide-bodied aircraft, each powered by three of the new 20-tonne engines — two wing-mounted and one in the tail.

These are the McDonnell Douglas DC-10 and Lockheed TriStar. There are several models, of which some can accommodate up to 400 passengers.

The fourth wide-bodied aeroplane is the European Airbus Industrie A300. This is powered by two General Electric CF6 turbofans each giving 23,135 kg (51,000 lb) thrust, and seats about 250 passengers. The A300 entered service in May 1974 and is regarded as the quietest of all the large transport aeroplanes.

These four very big wide-bodied aeroplanes will be carrying a high percentage of the world's air traffic over the remaining years of this century, and further development could extend their lives well into the next.

Supersonic transports

Since the introduction of jet transports, speeds of 800-960 km/h (500-600 mph) have been common. But in Britain, France, the USA and the USSR much effort has also been put into producing supersonic transports (SSTs) capable of flying at more than twice the speed of sound — Mach 2 or over 2,090 km/h (1,300 mph). The US design competition involved Boeing, Lockheed and North American, and three engine companies. Boeing and General Electric were finally chosen to produce a 250/350-passenger aeroplane with four GE engines beneath the tailplane. A wing spanning 53 m (174 ft) was designed to pivot so that it was swept back 20° at low speed and 72° when supersonic. A full-scale mock-up was built, but the design was scrapped in favour of a delta-wing layout and then the whole project was cancelled.

Britain's BAC and Aérospatiale of France worked together to produce the Concorde, a narrow-delta design powered by four Olympus engines rated at 17,410 kg (38,300 lb) each. The long, slender fuselage accommodates about 100 passengers and the nosecone is drooped during take-off and landing to improve the pilots' view.

Concordes are produced on two lines, one at Bristol and the other at Toulouse. The first flight took place on March 2, 1969, and after a long test programme British Airways and Air France inaugurated supersonic services simultaneously on January 21, 1976, when one aircraft left London for Bahrain and another took off from Paris for Dakar and Rio de Janeiro. The Concorde has a length of 62.17 m (204 ft) and a take-off weight of 176,453 kg (389,000 lb). This very advanced aeroplane cuts flight times by more than half and crosses the North Atlantic in just over three hours. But in spite of earlier interest, total orders remain at four for Air France and five for British Airways. The Soviet Union has built the very similar Tupolev Tu-144, which actually flew before the Concorde on the last day of 1968. One Tu-144 was lost in an accident during the 1973 Paris Air Show, but the type began operating cargo services between Moscow and Alma Ata in December 1975. By autumn 1976 there was no definite news of its having entered passenger service.

Lack of space prevents inclusion here of the short-lived development of transport flying-boats since 1945. Nor is it possible to cover the transport helicopters or such third-level equipment as the Twin Otter (more than 500 sold) and the Britten-Norman Islander and Trislander (700 orders). But a brief description must be given of Soviet transport aircraft development.

Soviet air transport

In the immediate post-war years the Soviet Union's air transport fleet lagged far behind the West's, with

Above left The European Airbus Industrie A300 is the
fourth and latest wide-bodied aeroplane, and has been in
service since May 1974.

Above The Boeing 747SP (Special Purpose), a short-body,
long-range aircraft, developed from the original 747 model.

a selection of unsophisticated Li-2s, Il-12s, Il-14s and small single-engined aircraft forming the Aeroflot fleet up to 1956. But in 1953 a major programme was begun to produce more modern aircraft. The first result was the Tupolev Tu-104, a major achievement when it is remembered that the Soviet Union had completely missed the aircraft generation represented by the West's two and four-engined pressurized airliners.

The Tu-104 used the wings, tail, undercarriage and engine installation of the Tu-16 bomber. This speeded the design and test phases, and the type first flew on June 17, 1955. It was a low-wing monoplane with sweptback wings and tail surfaces, retractable nosewheel undercarriage and press-urized cabins for 50 passengers. The two 6,750 kg (14,881 lb) Mikulin RD-3 or AM-3 turbojets were located in the wing roots, and there were tail parachutes for emergency braking. Cruising speed was 750-800 km/h (466-497 mph). The Tu-104 went into service with Aeroflot on the Moscow-Omsk-Irkutsk route on September 15, 1956. About 20 Tu-104s were built, followed by the 70-passenger Tu-104A and 100-passenger Tu-104B. It is thought that more than 200 aircraft of the series were produced, many of which are still in service 20 years later.

Four new Soviet types appeared in 1957. One, the four-engined Tu-110 development of the Tu-104, failed to enter service. The others were each powered by four turboprops and were destined to play a major role in Soviet air transport. First to enter service, in April 1959, was the low-wing Ilyushin Il-18 with four 4,000 hp Ivchenko AI-20 engines. Initially fitted out for 80 passengers, its performance and capacity was continuously developed and many operated with 110 seats. The Il-18 cruised at 625-650 km/h (388-404 mph) and more than 800 were built. The type formed the backbone of Aeroflot's fleet and large numbers remain in service.

Entering service three months after the Il-18 was the Antonov An-10, of similar capacity but with a high-mounted wing and an undercarriage designed for operation from rough surfaces. A large number of An-10s and improved An-10As were operated, only to be withdrawn following a major fatal accident in May 1972. The An-12 freight version, with rear under-fuselage loading doors, is still in large-scale civil and military use.

The fourth type flown in 1957 was the biggest

and fastest propeller-driven airliner ever to go into service. The Tu-114 had a 51.1 m (167 ft 7¾ in) span, four 12,000/15,000 hp NK-12 turboprops, a maximum take-off weight of 175,000 kg (385,805 lb) and accommodation for up to 220 passengers, although 120-170 was more common. The Tu-114 cruised at up to 770 km/h (478 mph) and had a range of about 8,950 km (5,560 miles). It entered service in April 1961, operated trans-Siberian services and opened the Soviet Union's first North Atlantic routes. Only about 30 were built.

Having provided the necessary medium- and long-range equipment, the Soviet Union next turned to aircraft for the shorter routes, introducing the twin-turboprop Antonov An-24 and the twin-turbofan Tu-124 in October 1962. The An-24 closely resembles the Fokker F.27, and well over 800 are believed to be in service. The Tu-124 was a three-quarter-scale Tu-104 with 44-56 seats, but only about 100 were built. From it was developed the somewhat larger Tu-134 with rear-mounted engines, which went into service in September 1967. The Tu-134 has been built in large numbers and some have been exported.

Aeroflot was also keen to introduce an intercontinental jet to replace the Tu-114. This resulted in the 168/186-seat Ilyushin Il-62, which, with its four rear-mounted engines and T-tail, resembles the British VC10. The Il-62 entered service in March 1967; more than 100 are in service with Aeroflot, and small numbers have been exported mainly to East European airlines.

A unique Soviet transport began operation in September 1968. This was the small 24/32-passenger Yak-40 powered by three rear-mounted AI-25 turbofans. Designed for short stages and operations from rough surfaces, it has no real Western counterpart. It appears that more than 800 have been built, some of which have been exported to several German, Greek, Italian and Afghan airlines.

Having had long service out of its first-generation turbine aircraft, the Soviet Union came up with the 126/152-seat Tu-154 as a replacement. In the same category as the Boeing 727-200, it has three rear-mounted NK-8 turbofans and cruises at about 900 km/h (560 mph). The type entered service in November 1971 and some have been exported. But the type has suffered a number of accidents and those supplied to Egypt were soon returned to the Soviet Union.

In the near future the Soviet Union will have the 350-passenger four-engined Il-86, nearing completion in the autumn of 1976, and the 120-passenger three-engined Yak-42, which made its first flight in March 1975.

Some specialized cargo operations are handled by the high-wing four-jet Il-76, which has a 40-tonne payload and first appeared at the Paris Air Show in 1971. Another very big Soviet freighter made its Western debut at the 1965 Paris Show, having flown at the beginning of that year. This was the An-22, which weighs 250,000 kg (551,160 lb) and is powered by four 15,000 hp NK-12 turboprops. Though it has carried loads of more than 80 tonnes and has been used on a few international flights with special cargo, there is no evidence that it is in regular Aeroflot service on Soviet Union domestic routes.

Chapter 7

HELICOPTERS AND LIGHT AIRCRAFT

THE development of rotary-winged aircraft, helicopters and gyrocopters, proceeded at a much slower pace than the fixed-wing variety. Early rotorcraft experiments had limited success. The real breakthrough came with the work of Juan de la Cierva in the mid-twenties and thirties.

Gyrocopters

De la Cierva identified the principle of the gyrocopter and called his aircraft 'autogiros', a trade name which is used only when referring to Cierva machines. Subsequently, manufacturers such as Wg Cdr Kenneth Wallis in Britain and the American Igor Bensen have used the form 'autogyro' for their designs. The gyrocopter is something of a hybrid of the conventional fixed-wing aircraft and the helicopter. Often the gyrocopter and helicopter are confused or mistaken for one another, making it useful to distinguish between the two types of rotary-winged aircraft.

The gyrocopter derives most of its lift in flight from rotors rotating freely in the horizontal plane. It relies on conventional airscrews to propel it forward fast enough to keep the rotors turning, and is capable of flying at speeds at which conventional aircraft would stall. Each rotor blade has an aerofoil section similar to that of a normal wing, and since the rotor is freewheeling there are none of the torque problems common in helicopters.

A gyrocopter has a conventional airscrew and a tail unit, and is often provided with short, stubby wings to give additional lift and stability. A conventional helicopter has no propulsive airscrew but generally has a small rotor mounted at right-angles to the tail to counter torque effects and provide directional control. Some larger helicopters have two or more main rotors and do not therefore need tail rotors. Gyrocopter rotors are unpowered, being turned by the airflow passing over them in flight, while a helicopter's main and tail rotors are engine-driven. A helicopter can

Above left Royal Navy 'copters of the 1970s. From top to bottom: Westland Sea King, Wessex Mk3, Wessex Mk5, Wessex Mk1, the Lynx and the Wasp.

Above right Beagle Aircraft Ltd built 150 Pups before production came to an end in 1969. The type was available as a two or four seater.

hover, fly sideways and backwards, and land and take off vertically. A gyrocopter needs a short take-off run, although in a strong wind it can take off with very little run; it cannot climb or descend vertically. In full flight, the rotor blades of a helicopter tilt forwards, those of a gyrocopter backwards.

Cierva began his researches into the stalling characteristics of fixed-wing aircraft after a trimotor biplane which he built in 1918 stalled and crashed. He discovered that a rotary wing revolving freely would maintain sufficient lift whatever the forward speed, thus avoiding the stall. His first designs were disheartening. The first, the C-1, was uncontrollable and the next two had to be rebuilt several times. Cierva then built a small model

141

autogiro and discovered that the model flew well because the blades were flexible. Thus inspired, Cierva incorporated articulating rotors on his next design, the C-4. A few modifications later, Cierva finally took to the air near Madrid on January 9, 1923. These initial flights of just a few hundred metres were improved on very quickly, and by the end of the month Cierva had made a closed-circuit flight of 4 km (2½ miles) in 4 minutes.

In 1926 the Cierva Autogiro Company was founded in Great Britain to issue licences for autogiro construction. The year before, Cierva had presented his C-6 to the Air Ministry. An Avro 504K fuselage stripped of its wings, the C-6 featured a 36 ft-diameter four-bladed rotor mounted on a steel-tube pylon. A successful demonstration before the top brass at RAE Farnborough resulted in an order for two, which were constructed by A. V. Roe at Hamble in Hampshire.

In one of these machines, the C-8, Cierva became the first passenger to fly in a rotary-wing aircraft. During the next decade the Cierva-Avro partnership produced a variety of autogiros, of which the best known was the C-30. This was the first autogiro to have a direct-control rotor, which spun up to flying speed by means of a drive from the engine before being declutched for flight. Earlier

Above British built Cierva C.30s were licence built by A.V.Roe at Manchester during the 1930s. Some were later impressed into wartime service with the RAF.

Right The Flettner Fl 282 was used for convoy protection and reconnaissance. They operated from ships, usually at dusk or dawn.

rotors were often pre-spun with a piece of rope, or even by hand.

The C-30 also embodied a hanging stick for rotor control. It tilted the rotor head forwards or backwards for pitch changes, and sideways for turns. An open-cockpit two-seater, the C-30 became very popular with private pilots and flying clubs, being both cheap and easy to fly. The C-30 had a maximum speed of 177 km/h (110 mph) and a range of 460 km (285 miles).

Apart from A. V. Roe's output, autogiros were also being licence-built in France, Germany and America, and by such British companies as de Havilland, Short Brothers and Westland. Then, at the peak of his career and having moved on to pure helicopters, Cierva was killed in a flying accident, ironically in a fixed-wing aircraft. The KLM DC-2 in which he was travelling to Amsterdam crashed minutes after leaving Croydon in thick fog on December 9, 1936. His death marked the beginning of a decline in the autogiro fashion.

Pilots were more impressed by the superior performance and comfort of the wide range of fixed-wing private aircraft flooding on to the market, and although a few 'one-off' cabin autogiros with better performance were produced, production of the Cierva designs virtually stopped with the outbreak of World War II. Many civilian autogiros were impressed into RAF service to join a handful of Avro Rotors (the military variant of the C-30) as Army co-operation aircraft with No 529 Sqn, the RAF's one and only autogiro unit.

But elsewhere development continued vigorously. While Britain had been enjoying the heyday of the autogiro, Cierva's ideas had reached America. In 1929 US rights were sold to the Pitcairn organisation, which formed the Autogyro Company of America and in turn granted licences to the Kellett Aircraft Corporation. One of the Kellett types, the KD-1, was comparable to the C-30 but incorporated a number of refinements. It was an open-cockpit two-seater with performance superior

to that of the C-30. The cockpits were readily accessible and folding rotor blades afforded easy and cheaper storage. A KD-1 carried out the first scheduled autogyro airmail flight in the world shortly after making the first recorded rooftop landing at the opening of the Philadelphia Post Office in May 1935. A development of the KD-1 was evaluated and flown by the US Army, and a handful of the YO-60 military version were used as observation aircraft by that service during World War II. After the war Kellett, like Cierva, branched out into the pure helicopter field.

Two particularly interesting gyrocopter applications were developed during the Second World War. The German Focke-Achgelis company built a tiny motorless gyrocopter called the FA-330. Towed kite-fashion behind U-boats, it was used for spotting enemy shipping, effectively increasing the submarine's periscope height to 600 ft. Rotor diameter was 7.4 m (24 ft) and the pilot sat on a steel-tube structure that could be collapsed for easy stowage within the confines of a submarine.

143

Similar in concept was the British-built Rota-plane. A motorless gyrocopter designed for the Airborne Forces Experimental Establishment by Raoul Hafner, the Rotaplane was described as a controllable rotary-wing parachute capable of carrying a man and a Bren gun. It was planned to drop Rotaplanes from large transport aircraft at pre-determined vantage points for battlefield reconnaissance, but in the event the design never entered service. Like the German FA-330, the Rotaplane had a tubular structure, with the pilot seated just in front of the rotor pylon. The framework aft of the pylon was faired with a rubberized bag kept rigid by air rammed into it through a forward-facing scoop. Several versions of the Rotaplane were tested, towed behind jeeps or Tiger Moths. On at least one occasion a Rotaplane was towed up to nearly 4,000 ft before being released. But despite these successes, a change in Air Ministry policy spelt the end for this interesting project in 1943.

After World War II interest in the autogyro flagged as the more versatile helicopter began to compete for development time and money. But in the early 1950s the American Igor B. Bensen, founder of the Bensen Aircraft Corporation, turned his attention to Cierva's unpowered-rotor concept. After devoting several years to a series of gyro-gliders, he produced his first gyrocopter in 1957. The B-8M was even smaller than the German FA-330 and was powered by a 72 hp McCulloch engine giving a cruising speed of 97 km/h (60 mph). Bensen designed the B-8M for amateur construction, and simplicity was the byword. It was also very simple to fly, cruising at 24 km/h (15 mph) and landing at a mere 11 km/h (7 mph). Bensen's designs very quickly caught on, providing the private fliers of the 1950s with the kind of cheap, highly popular aviation also enjoyed today by hot-air balloonists and hang-glider pilots. Kits and plans sold by the hundred and various improvements have been incorporated in the latest models. The B-8MA has been developed for agricultural spraying and the B-8M Superbug has a twin-engine installation which allows the rotor to be spun up for take-off.

Since 1961 Britain's Wg Cdr K. H. Wallis has been experimenting with autogyros and has produced a series of highly sophisticated craft. He began by building and flying his own Bensen gyrocopters but has since refined the concept and patented a number of ideas of his own, including a device which permits 'hands-and-feet-off' flying. Wallis autogyros have been used in a number of interesting roles, being custom-built rather than turned out on a production line. A WA-117 flew over Loch Ness during the 1970 observations, others starred in a James Bond film, and another was used by a British police force in the search for a missing person.

Helicopters

For centuries man has been intrigued by the idea of lifting himself vertically into the air without taking a run at it first. Although visionaries like Leonardo da Vinci and Britain's Sir George Cayley nibbled intelligently at the problem, it was not until 1907 that real progress was made. In that year the French mechanic Cornu built a helicopter based on experiments he had made with models. His design centred on a 24 hp Antoinette engine driving two 6.2 m (20 ft) rotors by means of belts. The pilot sat behind the engine on a four-wheeled V structure, and the whole machine, including pilot weighed 260 kg (573 lb). On November 13, 1907, Cornu's apparatus strained to a height of about one foot, remaining there for 20 seconds. Although the Frenchman's frail and unstable craft survived for only a short while afterwards, the helicopter had arrived.

Just as the autogyro owes its existence to Juan de la Cierva, so the helicopter has one undisputed progenitor, the Russian Igor Sikorsky. Beginning in 1900, he experimented unsuccessfully, producing early models which featured contra-rotating rotors to eliminate torque. But his first helicopter failed to leave the ground and the second could only lift itself *sans* pilot, and so the disappointed Sikorsky turned his attentions to fixed-wing aircraft. It was not until thirty years later that he took up his old interest, but by then he was resident in the USA, having settled there in 1919, and he had revised his ideas about torque and stability problems.

His first new helicopter was the VS-300, with a single main rotor and a small torque-opposing tail

rotor. The VS-300 changed configuration many times before making its first successful flight in May 1940. In April 1941 Sikorsky fitted flotation bags to this helicopter, which shortly afterwards was credited with the first American amphibious helicopter flight. The VS-300 paved the way for the R-4, the first helicopter to be produced in quantity for the US Army Air Force, US Navy and the RAF. In service with the RAF the R-4 was called the Hoverfly, flying with No 529 Sqn on radar-calibration duties and replacing the Avro Rotor in this role.

The R-5 was followed by one of the first great helicopters, the S-51. Sikorsky's first commercial helicopter, the S-51 was also the first to be licensed by the American Civil Aviation Authority for commercial operations. The S-51 and subsequent Sikorsky designs were licence-built in Britain by Westland at Yeovil. Production rights for the S-51 were acquired in 1947, and both civil and military versions were produced. The military version, ordered by the RAF, was named the Dragonfly and was used for casualty-evacuation duties until finally withdrawn from service in 1956. But even then the S-51 was far from finished — Westland redesigned and updated the basic airframe, and offered the resulting Widgeon to commercial operators. Westland also acquired rights to the S-55, the S-58 and the S-61, naming them Whirl-wind, Wessex and Sea King respectively. The

Above left Wing Commander Ken Wallis's series of autogyros began in 1961 with the WA-116. A full range of gyrocopters has since been developed.

Top Vought-Sikorsky developed the experimental XR-4 in 1941. It was powered by a 165 hp Warner engine. The final service variant was the R-4B.

Above The Bensen B-8 series of gyrocopters are available in several forms including a kit.

Whirlwind was offered to civilian operators but it was with the Royal Navy and the air-sea rescue services that it came into its own. Such was the reliability of the Whirlwind that the type was chosen for the Queen's Flight. The S-58 derivative is the Wessex, in service with the Royal Navy and the RAF. Wessex variants include the Mk 60, a civil version capable of carrying ten passengers in airliner accommodation and up to 16 for pipeline or oil-rig support. The Sea King serves with the Royal Navy as an advanced anti-submarine helicopter. It is capable of air-to-surface strikes, plus search and rescue, casualty evacuation and other secondary roles.

Westland also built the Scout, a compact five/six-seat general-purpose helicopter originally designed by Saunders Roe at Cowes in 1957. It first flew in 1958 and production for the British Army was taken up by Westland when Saunders Roe became a division of that company. A version for

Above In 1957 Westland flew their developed version of the American Sikorsky S-58. It was named Wessex and later versions were powered by two coupled Gnome engines. A civil version is the Wessex 60.

Right The Westland Wasp anti-submarine helicopter, capable of carrying two homing torpedoes, originated as the private venture P.531 and went into service with the Royal Navy in 1963.

the Royal Navy, the Wasp, is powered by a 710 shp Rolls-Royce Nimbus engine. The Wasp has a folding tail and a special swivelling landing gear designed for deck operations, and is the first helicopter to operate extensively from platforms aboard the Royal Navy's frigates and smaller vessels. It can carry two Mk 44 torpedoes and air-to-surface missiles, and can perform search and rescue, training and reconnaissance duties.

Germany was amongst the pre-war leaders in helicopter development and in 1937 the Focke 61 designed by Prof H. K. J. Focke set up a series of

world records, among them an endurance record of 1 hour 20 minutes 49 seconds. This twin-rotored craft, with a fuselage not unlike that of a scaled-up Cierva C.30 (for which Focke had earlier been granted a construction licence), was flown by Hanna Reitsch, the distinguished lady pilot. On one of her most publicised flights in the Focke 21 she flew inside Berlin's Deutschland-Halle in 1938, dramatically demonstrating the type's manoeuvrability.

Another German pioneer in this field was Anton Flettner. After experimenting with both autogyros and helicopters, he designed and produced the first helicopter with intermeshing contra-rotating rotors, the FL-265. The first two were destroyed when their blades collided, but four others were tested from the decks of cruisers and provided much valuable information for the FL-262. This was a greatly improved version, again with intermeshing rotors, which was intended for operation from cruisers on anti-submarine patrols. But for an air raid on the Flettner factories, the FL-282 would have gone into full wartime production. In the event, only 22 of the original order for 1,000 were completed before the war ended.

Immediately after the end of World War II helicopter technology mushroomed. Although the United States had the most prolific output, Great Britain, France, Italy and the USSR made great strides. Italy's Agusta has been active in aviation since 1907 but it was not until 1957 that this company embarked on helicopter production. Agusta built the American Bell 47 under licence, turning out 1,000 examples in the first ten years. The company's activities are currently divided between licence-built American helicopters and a number of home-grown designs, the latest of which is the A.109 Hirundo.

Igor Sikorsky apart, Russia can boast another helicopter pioneer — Boris Yuriev, the originator of the classic helicopter configuration of main rotor and anti-torque tail rotor. Today the Soviet Union's leading helicopter exponents are the Mil and Kamov design bureaux. Nikolai Ilitch Kamov began experimenting with autogyros and helped produce Russia's first autogyro, the KASKR I, in 1930. Mikhail Mil's Mi-1 was the first Soviet helicopter to enter series production. In 1971 the gigantic Mi-12 caused a sensation at the Paris Air Show, where it appeared in the West for the first time. This massive helicopter is powered by four 6,500 shp Soloviev D-25VF free-turbine engines, and has two rotors 35.7 m (114 ft 10 in) in diameter and an all-up weight of 105,000 kg (231,500 lb). With a payload of 33,400 kg (78,000 lb) the Mi-12 has a range of just over 480 km (300 miles). On August 6, 1969, an early Mi-12 climbed to 7,398 ft with a payload of 39,890 kg (88,636 lb).

Twenty years earlier, a British machine held the heavy lift record for a while. A Cierva W.11 Air Horse, an experimental 24-seater with three rotors 14.6 m (47 ft) in diameter and driven by a single Rolls-Royce Merlin engine, lifted from Eastleigh in England at an all-up weight of 6,300 kg (14,000 lb). Of the two Air Horses built, one crashed when the rotor hub failed and the other was put into long-term storage. At the other end of the scale, the Cierva company was developing a small two-seat helicopter called the Skeeter. Development and production was taken up by Saro and the Skeeter was eventually ordered into Army and RAF service. It had a top speed of 163 km/h (101 mph) and was powered by a de Havilland Gipsy Major 30 engine.

The first British-designed helicopter to enter RAF service was the Bristol Sycamore, the prototype of which first flew in July 1947, more than a year before the Skeeter. The larger of the two types, the Sycamore was employed on search-and-rescue duties and versions served with the Army and the RAF. The Sycamore could carry three passengers, or two stretchers, and a crew of two. It was powered by a 550 hp Alvis Leonides 73 engine giving it a top speed of 205 km/h (127 mph).

The helicopter's ability to hover over any given spot, and put down and pick up loads in areas inaccessible to other vehicles, makes it a perfect rescue/recovery craft. US Vertol CH-47 Chinooks retrieved hundreds of aircraft worth well over $3,000 million in Vietnam. In one flight a Chinook evacuated 147 people, compared with a design capability of 44 troops or 24 litters. Designed for all-weather operations, the CH-47 first flew in 1961 and entered service with the US Army late in 1962. One version is equipped with an external cargo hook capable of lifting 7,257 kg (16,000 lb). The CH-47 can also carry a complete artillery section, including two howitzers, ammunition and gun crews.

In its latest military role the helicopter is armed and armoured for 'gunship' operations. Although helicopters are capable of nipping in and out of battle zones inaccessible to other vehicles, they are extremely vulnerable while hovering to take on or discharge cargo or personnel. It was to provide protection under these circumstances that the Bell Model 209 HueyCobra was conceived. The first example flew in September 1965, and a year later the HueyCobra was ordered by the US Army. An impressive array of armament includes Miniguns (six-barrelled machine guns loaded with up to 8,000 rounds) and a variety of rockets and grenades mounted on underwing pylons. The US Marine Corps operates a twin-engined version of the HueyCobra, and in 1971 Bell announced the Model 309 Kingcobra, capable of operating anti-

The Bell AH-1 Huey Cobra armed helicopter began service in Vietnam in 1967. The AH-1 has an under-nose gun turret. Attachments below the stub wings carry mini-gun or rocket pods.

armour missions in the worst of weather and terrain. The Kingcobra is well suited to this close-support role — its small size and very narrow profile, achieved by seating the pilot and gunner in tandem, make it easy to conceal behind trees or under camouflage nets.

The helicopter gunship of the 1980s is about to emerge from the US Army's Advanced Attack Helicopter (AAH) competition. Bell and Hughes have been selected to build two AAH prototypes

each, plus an airframe for ground testing. Bell's YAH-63 is a twin-turbine helicopter capable of engaging enemy armour by day or night in all weathers. It is armed with anti-tank missiles, a three-barrelled 30 mm cannon mounted under the nose, and folding-fin rockets launched from beneath the stub wings.

The Bell company also figures prominently in the civil helicopter field. Apart from the enormously successful Bell 47, which remained in production for 25 years, the company has produced the Model 206 JetRanger series. This five-seat turbine-powered helicopter first flew in 1965 and production began in 1967. Military versions were also produced — the Sea Ranger for the Navy, and the Kiowa light observation model for the US Army. In 1971 Bell offered the more powerful JetRanger II, with a maximum level speed of 225 km/h (140 mph). 1973 saw the first proposals for the LongRanger, a six-seat general-purpose civil

machine that entered production in 1975. This version represented a quantum improvement in passenger comfort standards. Its Noda-Matic rotor-mounting system eliminates the vibration so long associated with helicopters, utilizing the principle which states that a beam subjected to vertical vibration develops waveform flexing. In such a beam, nodal points equidistant from the centre have no relative motion. Bell has connected the LongRanger's fuselage and rotor system at such nodal points to provide an extremely smooth ride.

Today, aerospace companies have combined their resources to collaborate on specific projects. In 1967 an Anglo-French agreement resulted in co-operation between Westland and Aérospatiale on the design and production of the SA.341 Gazelle. This five-seat all-purpose helicopter is powered by two Turboméca Astazou III turbo-shafts giving a maximum cruising speed of 310 km/h (192 mph) at sea level. Also in quantity production under the agreement are the troop-carrying Puma and the Lynx utility and anti-submarine helicopter.

Lightplanes
The light aircraft has always been somewhat overshadowed in aviation. Fighters, bombers and airliners tend to hog the limelight, yet there are probably more aircraft in this class than there are in all the others put together. The lightplane is the

equivalent of the motor car or the yacht, as useful for leisure activities as it is for business.

One of the earliest devotees of private flying and all it had to offer was Claude Grahame-White, a wealthy young businessman who made a name for himself in the motor industry at the turn of the century, as well as being something of a property dealer. He realized that aviation had arrived and bought land for the London Aerodrome at Hendon. There he built aeroplanes, started a flying club and school, and organized unforgettable race meetings during most summer weekends just before World War I.

A natural showman who tried wholeheartedly to get Britain air-minded, Grahame-White was also a very accomplished pilot who could really use his aircraft. The pages of *Flight* and *The Aeroplane* were full of his flights around England. He would regularly fly into tea parties organized by friends, landing on the lawn wearing flying goggles and reversed hat, and no doubt dressed to kill. In those days flying was regarded more as an eccentric sport than as a practical means of transport.

The end of World War I spawned a surplus of pilots, aeroplanes and flying circuses, and pleasure-flight companies mushroomed everywhere. One of the most popular aircraft for these purposes was the ubiquitous Avro 504K trainer. They were cheap to buy, spares were abundant and pilots came two-a-penny. These little companies provided many thousands of people with their first

taste of aviation, taking them for quick five-bob flips from local fields and around the town. A few aerobatics cost a little more, and they were back on the ground within five minutes.

But for some reason people were not interested in learning to fly themselves, perhaps because it was so very expensive. A one-hour flying lesson could cost £7 in the early 1920s, and a private pilot's licence cost anything up to £150 to obtain. But apart from other war-surplus aircraft, such as the S.E.5 and Bristol Fighter, there were few other training aircraft available.

In 1922 the *Daily Mail* sponsored the first gliding competition ever held in Britain. Contestants were invited to construct their own gliders and fly them at Itfield in Sussex. The event attracted over 30 entrants, many of whom showed up with devices which had no chance whatsoever of flying. One of the more successful entries came from the de Havilland company, based at Hatfield in Hertfordshire, which tried its luck with two D.H.52 single-seat gliders. Though one of the D.H.52s broke up in the air and the other was scrapped soon after the competition, Itfield was to remain an important landmark for de Havilland.

The Itfield contest led to a series of motor-glider trials at Lympne in Kent, the first of which was held in 1923. Once again, the *Daily Mail*, anxious to keep up its aviation connection, offered large money prizes after having already spent £40,000 on contest sponsorship. Although other organizations also offered prizes, the competition was known as the *Daily Mail* Trials. De Havilland entered two D.H.53 Humming Birds, basically similar to the D.H.50 but powered by 750 cc Douglas motorcycle engines. Although neither won any prizes, one of them managed to fly 95 km(59 miles) on 2.2 litres (one gallon) of petrol. After the contest another D.H.53 flew from Lympne to Brussels, covering the 242 km (150 miles) in four hours and using just ten shillings-worth of petrol.

From the D.H.53 was developed what is widely regarded as the world's most famous light aeroplane — the Moth. A two-seat biplane originally powered by a 60 hp ADC Cirrus I, the Moth could

cruise at 129 km/h (80 mph) for 515 km (320 miles) at an all-up weight of 350 kg (764 lb). Folding wings meant that it could be hangared cheaply in garages or garden sheds. The Moth emerged from its chrysalis in 1925 and for the next decade in Britain every light aircraft was known as a 'Moff', whatever it was.

The most popular variant was the Gipsy Moth, powered by a Gipsy I or II engine of 100/120 hp. Pioneering aviator Amy Johnson immortalized the type when she flew her Gipsy Moth *Jason* from Croydon to Australia in May 1930. This epic flight — the first England-Australia solo by a woman — inspired the man in the street. 'If a young slip of an office girl can do that . . .', he thought.

Inevitably, other companies jumped on the bandwagon. Avro produced the very similar Avian, built in vast numbers and also highly successful. Designed originally for the 1926 *Daily Mail* Lympne Trials, the Avian made record flights to all parts of the world. Blackburn offered the Bluebird, again entered for the *Daily Mail* Trials, in 1924. It was moderately successful for the Leeds company, with about 80 being built. But good as these and other contenders for the burgeoning lightplane market were, none of them could oust the Moth from its premier position.

In the event, it took the dawning of the monoplane age to do that. Pilots were demanding new standards of cabin comfort, calling for the warmth and protection of an enclosed cockpit. After all, not everyone wanted to fly in clothes more suited to an Everest expedition. They also wanted faster

mounts — there were records to be broken, races to be won, and girlfriends to impress. The de Havilland company responded with the Puss Moth, a high-wing, three-seat monoplane capable of cruising at 177 km/h (110 mph). Its success story was to be repeated many times over the next decade as a family of Moth types emerged from the de Havilland stable.

The Hatfield manufacturer's main rival in this field was the Miles company at Reading. During the 1930s Miles produced a long line of elegant low-wing monoplanes which became very popular tourers, racers and general-purpose aircraft. Miles machines were consistent King's Cup air-racing winners and finalists, as were their de Havilland rivals.

Meanwhile, across the Atlantic, another company was making an indelible mark on the history of the lightplane. The Taylor Brothers Aircraft Corporation was set up by the brothers C. G. and Gordon Taylor in the late 1920s to build the Chummy, a two-seat, side-by-side parasol monoplane powered by a 90 hp engine. It was planned to sell the Chummy at $4,000 a copy, a lot of money in those days. But then the 1929 stock-market crash left the company in dire straits, with many of its would-be customers bankrupted overnight. Salvation appeared in the form of oilman William Piper, who became a director of the company.

Taylor Brothers' relief from financial travail was brief, however, and in 1931 the company went bankrupt. All assets, including the rights to the new Model E-2 Cub, were bought by Piper. From

Right A few D.H. Tiger Moths were fitted with floats and for many years one was the only British registered floatplane, a far cry from the golden years of flying boats.

Top far right The Beech Model V35 Bonanza, with its characteristic V tail, first appeared in the United States of America in 1947 and was still in production, in updated form, in the 1970s.

Above far right The French Pierre Robin DR 253 Regent four/five seat tourer is just one of a large range of similar aircraft produced to challenge American domination of the European market.

the ashes rose the Taylor Aircraft Company, formed by Piper and the brothers to build an improved version of the E-2 with totally enclosed cockpit. Then, in 1937, there rolled out of the Taylor sheds the first example of the archetypal lightplane — the immortal J-3 Cub. That year the company became the Piper Aircraft Corporation and Cubs began to flood off the production lines. The Cub was built in thousands right through the war until production was finally cut back in 1947, when the forecast light-aviation boom failed to materialize. The PA-18 Super Cub, an updated, more powerful version of the J-3, appeared in 1949 and was still coming off the lines at the rate of one every two days in the mid-1970s.

Ironically, company founder C. G. Taylor played no part in this staggering success story. After the 1937 company name-change Taylor left to form Taylorcraft Aircraft Corporation of Alliance, Ohio. There he produced a light aircraft similar to the Cub, a high-wing, two-seat cabin monoplane which became very popular in America. In 1938 a subsidiary company, Taylorcraft Aeroplanes (England) Ltd, was formed in Britain to build the Taylorcraft Plus C. The first of these appeared in 1938, winning an Air Ministry order. Large numbers of the type, designated Plus D, served in the liaison and communications roles with the RAF. After the war many Taylorcraft were civilianized, and in 1946 the company changed its name to

Auster Aircraft Ltd and moved to Rearsby in Leicestershire.

During World War II there was no civil flying in Britain. Many private aircraft were impressed into RAF service and flown on communications duties. Then, when peace returned, history repeated itself with a glut of pilots and aircraft. But money and petrol were in equally short supply, and it was a year or two before the light-aircraft industry found its feet.

Among the demobbed types was the D.H. Tiger Moth, which combined the Puss Moth's inverted engine with the airframe of the ultimate D.H.60, the 60T Moth Trainer. The RAF had ordered the type in vast batches before and during the war, as had a number of flying clubs in the late 1930s. So many Tigers were available after the war that even in the mid-1950s they were being offered for sale at £1,000 a pair.

The late 1940s saw the debut of another aircraft tailored to the needs of the British private owner and flying club. It offered cabin comfort, three or four seats, higher performance, and it was a monoplane. The first Autocrat came off the newly formed Auster company's line in time to make the first post-war private flight on January 1, 1946, the day that civil flying resumed in Britain. The Autocrat was to the 1950s and 1960s what the Tiger Moth had been to the 1940s, and the Gipsy Moth to the 1930s.

Miles Aircraft continued to produce light aircraft after the war, one of the most popular being the Messenger, a low-wing, single-engined, all-wooden four-seater of moderate performance. At the same time, vast numbers of Miles Magister open-cockpit trainers were being demobbed and offered on the civil market. Like the Tiger Moths, they were snapped up by clubs and private pilots, and were to provide many with cheap (if spartan) flying until the early 1960s. Miles also designed a smooth little twin-engined monoplane tourer called the Gemini. Those British private pilots who crossed the Channel and the North Sea craved the reassurance provided by the second engine, and saw the extra speed as a bonus. The Gemini therefore became quite popular and about 170 were built before Miles Aircraft collapsed in 1947.

The 1950s saw the British light aircraft industry in the doldrums. True enough, Auster was churning out various types by the hundreds, but right up into the 1960s most of Britain's light aircraft were wood-built and advancing in years.

In America it was a different story. Light aviation in the 1960s was big business, and the three major producers of light aircraft — Beechcraft, Cessna and Piper — ran their production lines in almost the same way as automobile

giants like Ford and General Motors. All three currently offer the full range of light aircraft, ranging from two-seat single-engined trainer/tourers through to the large twin-engined executive machines operated by air-taxi operators and feeder airlines. Typical of the first category is the enormously popular Piper Cherokee. At peak production 15 of these aircraft came off the production line at Vero Beach, California, every day, and the 10,000th Cherokee was delivered only 6½ years after the type first went into production in February 1961. Similarly, Cessna's equally successful 150 and 172 equip flying clubs and schools throughout the world. In May 1962 Cessna became the first company to deliver its 100,000th aircraft.

Beechcraft first flew its Beech Bonanza, a V-tailed, low-wing four-seater, in 1945. By January 1972 9,300 had been delivered and the type remains in production in steadily updated form.

In the early 1960s Britain lifted her light-aircraft import embargo and admitted a flood of foreign aircraft, mostly from Beech, Cessna and Piper. Within a few years the entire light-aviation scene in Britain had changed, with all-metal aircraft replacing the ageing wooden museum-pieces that had sustained British private flying for so many years.

The home industry made one notable effort to stem the influx of imported equipment. In April 1962 Beagle Aircraft was formed, based principally on Miles and Auster interests. A number of promising designs took to the air, including the Terrier, Airedale, Pup and the Beagle B.206 seven-seat executive aircraft. The Terrier was little more than an updated Auster, but the Airedale was a new design closely resembling the American high-wing four-seaters available at the time. The Pup was a two/four-seat, low-wing single-engined aircraft, aerobatic and very pleasing to the eye. For a while things looked rosy on the home front, but in 1969 the British Government withdrew financial support and Beagle fell into the hands of the Receiver. Once again, the Americans, and more recently the French, had it their own way.

Only survivor of the Beagle crash was the Pup, which lives on as the Bulldog military basic trainer. In production at Scottish Aviation's Prestwick plant in Scotland, the Bulldog is the RAF's basic trainer and has been ordered by a number of overseas buyers. A retractable-undercarriage version, the Bullfinch, is under development.

Page numbers in italics refer to pictures.
Numbers are indexed as if they were spelled out.

ACKNOWLEDGMENTS

The publishers wish to thank the
following individuals and
organizations for their kind
permission to reproduce the
photographs in this book:

Aeritalia Sp. A. 89
Air B.P. 21 above
Air France 120 above, 128
Air Ministry 35, 40–41
Air Portraits 81, 104 above
Associated Press endpapers
Bell Helicopter
  Company 150–151
Boeing Company 51 above, 53,
  56, 56–57, 82 above left and
  right, 82–83 below, 94, 95
  above, 113 centre, 121 above,
  122–123, 123 below, 124
British Aircraft Corporation 64
  above, 113 below, 120 below,
  132, 148
Charles Brown 70–71, 78
Consolidated Vultee
  Aircraft 112 below
Daily Telegraph Colour
  Library 32
Dassault-Breguet Aviation 87
  above, 88 below
Douglas Aircraft
  Company 50–51
R. Fahey 104 below
Flight International 142, 144
Fokker-VFW 134
Arthur Gibson 126–127
James Gilbert 26–27, 27 above
W. Gordon-Davis 14
Hawker-Siddeley Aviation
  Ltd. 107, 118
The John Hillelson Agency
  Ltd. 15 above
Leslie Hunt 61 below, 62, 63
  above and below, 64 below
Imperial War Museum 33, 34
  above and below, 36, 38, 65, 76
Howard Levy 24 above, 25
  above, 28–29, 30 below, 145
  below, 152, 153 centre and
  below
Lockheed Aircraft
  Corporation 125 below

Lufthansa 136
Mansell Collection 6–7, 20
Harold Martin 75
Martin and Kelman 144
Otto Menge 79
Ministry of Defence (Crown
  Copyright) 102
David Mondey 92–93
K. McDonough 49 below
Port of New York Authority 138
Northrop Corporation 87 below,
  90–91
Pan Am 129
Richard Pike 141
Popperfoto 84–85
Herbert Rittmeyer 1
John Rigby 2–3, 22–23
N. B. Rivett 30–31
Rockwell International
  Corporation 91 below
Royal Air Force 103
Royal Navy 140–141
Saab-Scania Aktiebolag 88
  above
K. Sissons 154
South African Airways 125
  above
John Stroud 111, 112 above,
  130–131, 130 below, 133, 135,
  137, 139
John W. R. Taylor 8, 10, 11, 16,
  17, 19 below, 21 below, 24–25
  below, 28 above and below, 30
  above, 34 centre, 37, 39, 42–43,
  44 above and below, 45, 46, 47,
  48, 49 above, 52, 54–55, 58–59,
  60, 61 above, 64 centre, 66, 67,
  68–69, 68 below, 69 above,
  72–73 above and below, 74, 77,
  80, 86, 92, 95 below, 96, 98, 99,
  100, 101, 105, 106, 108, 109,
  113 above, 114, 115 above and
  below, 116, 117, 119 above, 121
  below, 145 above, 149, 153
  above, 155 above and below,
  157 above and below
U.S. Army Photo 12–13
U.S. Navy Photo 18–19
John Warwick 9
Mick West 55 above
Westland Helicopters Ltd. 146,
  147

PDO 83-1126